PETER SELG was born
studied medicine in Witt
Berlin. Until 2000, he worked as the head physician of
the juvenile psychiatry department of Herdecke
hospital in Germany. Dr Selg is now director of the Ita
Wegman Institute for Basic Research into Anthroposophy (Arlesheim, Switzerland) and professor of
medicine at the Alanus University of Arts and Social Sciences (Germany).
He lectures extensively and is the author of numerous books, including
The Figure of Christ, The Agriculture Course and Rudolf Steiner and
Christian Rosenkreutz. He is married with five children.

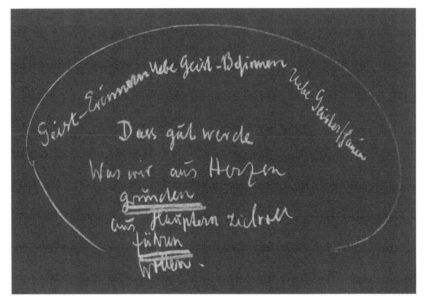

Practise spirit presence

Spirit recognition   Practise spirit beholding

That what we found
  From our hearts
  What we guide
  From our heads
  Will be good

Rudolf Steiner: blackboard illustration 30.12.1923 (volume XVII, plate 7, Rudolf Steiner Archive, Dornach).

Rudolf Steiner's Foundation Stone Meditation

and the Destruction of the Twentieth Century

PETER SELG

TEMPLE LODGE

Translated from German by Pauline Wehrle

Studies based on Rudolf Steiner's Meditations
Volume 1

For Eva

Temple Lodge Publishing
Hillside House, The Square
Forest Row, RH18 5ES

www.templelodge.com

Published by Temple Lodge 2012

Originally published in German under the title *Die Grundstein-Meditation Rudolf Steiners und die Zerstörungen des 20. Jahrhunderts* by Verlag des Ita Wegman Instituts in 2011

A catalogue record for this book is available from the British Library

ISBN 978 1 906999 41 4

Cover by Andrew Morgan incorporating photo of postwar Dresden
Typeset by DP Photosetting, Neath, West Glamorgan
Printed and bound by Berforts, Herts.

There is no doubt about it that right now the time has come when we human beings have reached decision time. We are going to have to make our minds up, once and for all, about tremendous issues, larger numbers of them. For in the course of the twentieth century [...] humanity will have arrived either at the grave of all civilization, or it will be facing the beginning of a new age in which those people who with their hearts and souls unite intelligence with spirituality, will fight on the side of Michael for the victory of the Michael powers.

Rudolf Steiner 1924[1]

Contents

Introduction

Life offers you two ways:
One leads to the realm of ideals, the other to death.
Friedrich Schiller[2]

The events in Japan of spring 2011 brought worldwide attention to the tremendous potential for disaster inherent in modern civilization. A great deal of what was experienced there, in the form of natural catastrophes caused by civilization such as the earthquake, tsunami and nuclear contamination, were, however, disasters already known to us for a considerable time — 'known', but not fully estimated: a distinction made by Hegel in his *Phenomenology of Spirit*. ('Because we *know of* something, we do not *estimate* it fully.')[3] Nor would anyone who had studied Eric Hobsbawm's fundamental historical study and balance sheet of the century, *Age of Extremes: The Short Twentieth Century 1914–1991* (London 1994), really be surprised by what happened in those weeks, resulting from the destructive developments of the nineteenth and twentieth centuries to which we still seldom give a thought, surrounded as we are by our Western economic prosperity and its apparently absolute materialistic values.

Shortly before the Japanese catastrophes, in January and February 2011, after innumerable journalists and authors had been smugly amusing themselves on the occasion of Rudolf Steiner's 150th birthday celebrations — about Steiner as the founder of anthroposophy in Middle Europe — and had even been presenting him in the media as the 'colourful genius', the relevance of Steiner's life's work was brought clearly to people's notice for a second time due to the sudden accumulation of disasters. Fritjof Capra, the physicist, philosopher and expert on the theory of systems, and known universally from his 1983 book *The Tao of Physics*, was not the first person to speak of the change of direction that needed to happen in people's thinking, for Rudolf Steiner already did so in his student days 100 years before, when he began working on Goethe's research into life phenomena, and from the age of 21 onwards (1882) worked on editing the other works of Goethe then available to the general public, in a most attractive form. Steiner's collected works, which he was producing right up until his death on 30 March 1925 against considerable contemporary resistance, was, after all, focussed on a new understanding of the human being, the world and creation, and stressed the need not to leave the future destiny of the Earth and humankind — including *all* the kingdoms of nature — solely in the hands of materialistic and technological 'progress', but to bring about a real humanising of civilization on the basis of both natural scientific *and* spiritual scientific knowledge. For Steiner the term 'spiritual science' did not mean the sum of all the non-natural-scientific fields of academic life, but original, methodical research work aimed at opening up human soul/spiritual dimensions of both the environment and the 'cosmos', so that these can become worthy companions to natural science; help to balance, correct and extend it. Rudolf Steiner had not the slightest doubt that this kind of spiritual science would not just supply abstract interpretations and con- tributions to debates on ethics, but would have to become *productive* in itself, by opening up new, practical ways of working among people and their various life activities and problems, from medicine to agriculture. The School of Spiritual Science formed by Steiner in Dornach near Basel, with its various faculties and associations, ought to work in this direction — researching, teaching, training, and putting things into practice.[4] Whilst the First World War was still in progress, Rudolf Steiner said in Ulm in April 1918:

> [...] In this present catastrophic time we are experiencing in a more terrible way than has ever happened before in the course of recorded history that humankind has come to an impasse, to a real dead end. And, seriously, they will only break free of it if they resolve to add to what they possess as physical culture, and of which they are so proud, an actual spiritual culture; one that is suitable for our present-day state of soul, and also for our time and the near future, and which is an integral part of the physical culture.
>
> We may resist as much as we want making these efforts to give the Earth a new spirituality, but the truth will under all circumstances have to be faced. Humanity is now living in a terribly disastrous time. If we are not prepared to resolve to bring in the spirituality meant here, then disasters of this kind will occur again and again, possibly with shorter and shorter intervals. These disasters and all their consequences will never be remedied with the methods we knew of before these catastrophes occurred. Those who still believe they will are not thinking in terms of the human evolutionary

process. And the length of time this catastrophic period will last —
even if we seem to bridge it over for a few years — will be until
humanity understands it in the only way possible, namely that it is a
sign that we human beings have to turn towards the spirit, the spirit
that should be filling our purely physical life with its vital force. For
many people today this may still be a bitter truth, a most uncom-
fortable one; but nevertheless it is the truth.[5]

What Rudolf Steiner meant by the expression 'to turn to the spirit', and
which became a familiar theme of his, was not an escape into theology,
esotericism or so-called 'spirituality', but the realization and civilizing
conversion of thinking into a kind of thinking that includes the realms of
soul/spiritual reality and does justice to them, e.g. by introducing a
knowledge of the incarnating process that exhibits concretely how spirit
works in matter. This was, and is, part and parcel of the endeavours to set
up new humanitarian social structures, ways of living and scientific
methods.

★

Rudolf Steiner formulated the so-called Foundation Stone meditation at
the end of 1923 at the Christmas Conference of the General Anthroposophical Society; it was the esoteric foundation of a large scale
endeavour to enable the School of Spiritual Science to become a reality at
a difficult time during the crisis years of the Weimar Republic, shortly
after the first attempted coup by Adolf Hitler.[6] ('For there is no doubt
about it that right now the time has arrived when we human beings have
reached decision time. We are going to have to make our minds up, once
and for all, about tremendous issues, large numbers of them.')[7] Rudolf
Steiner gave the Foundation Stone meditation to the members of the
Anthroposophical Society for their personal use, i.e. for the strengthening
of both their individual and their joint forces so that they would be able to
deal resolutely with the tasks awaiting them in the future. The Spiritual
Foundation Stone contains, in the words of Sergei O. Prokofieff, 'the
quintessence of the whole of anthroposophy'.[8]

   In view of the significance Rudolf Steiner gave to this great mantram
— and in view of the deep experiences many people had in experiencing
the real nature of the Foundation Stone meditation — in the course of the
succeeding decades it became the subject of numerous anthroposophical
studies and was finally also published. The studies were the expression of

many years of meditative experiences of the verses and illuminated this extraordinary treasure in the most varied ways. In particular, Willem Zeylmans van Emmichoven from Holland and the Russian Sergei O. Prokofieff produced fundamental studies towards a deeper understanding of the mantram[9], studies that showed us clearly that it actually did contain the 'quintessence of the whole of anthroposophy'. In an autobiographical review Prokofieff tells us how the words of the meditation affected him when he first encountered it in the German language:

> The sound of the German words of the Foundation Stone meditation opened up to me a completely new spirituality. The language I was hearing was as rich and spirit-filled as the sublime thoughts it conveyed. For the first time I experienced language and its content as an indivisible unity. For not only did the German language reveal itself to me at that moment as the only possible bearer of the abundant wisdom of the new Christian esotericism, but the content of the Foundation Stone meditation now appeared to me for the first time in all its cosmic and earthly power. [...]
>
> I felt [...] with my whole soul that there is only one other work clothed in human words that, seen spiritually, can compare with the Foundation Stone meditation: The John Gospel, or, to be precise, the prologue to it and the farewell speeches of Christ Jesus. It was clear to me right from the start: Both of them have sprung from the same source, originated from the one divine sphere of the cosmic Logos that embraces all worlds; they are a direct revelation of the living Christ.[10]

The doctor and psychologist Willem Zeylmans van Emmichoven had at the age of 30 taken part in the Christmas Conference, and was deeply moved by it; in fact he was shaken to the very core of his being. 'When at Christmas 1923 we came to Dornach for the founding of the General Anthroposophical Society I was, from the moment that Rudolf Steiner had performed the laying of the Foundation Stone, absolutely certain that we had witnessed a Mystery Act that applied to the whole of humanity; the first Mystery Act that was carried out absolutely publicly. Although the 800 people present were members they were so different from one another and on so many different levels of development that we have the right to say that this deed took place in full publicity. There were several people there, like me, who felt that they were experiencing their own birthday; I have now been born as a spiritual personality.'[11] Sergei O.

Prokofieff, on the other hand, heard the mantram of the Foundation Stone meditation in the German language more than five decades later, at Easter 1976 in Moscow, under quite different circumstances, at the age of 22, in a secret study circle within the Marx-Lenin dictatorship of the Soviet Union. During the half century between 1923, when Zeylmans experienced the Christmas Conference, and 1976, when Sergei O. Prokofieff encountered the mantram, the world had changed fundamentally and had, due to what happened in Germany, and by means of the very instrument of the German language, descended into immense depths. Writing in general terms about the fate of the language in the fascist twentieth century, Paul Celan said: 'The language itself, despite everything, remained unfallen. But it now had to go through an inability to give answers, through a terrible time of silence, through the thousand eclipses of death-dealing speech. It went through this, but said no word about what had happened; yet it *did* go through these happenings and was allowed to come to light again, enriched by it all.'[12]

The Foundation Stone meditation was also permitted to 'come to light again' after the end of World War Two and the fascist devastation; it had lost none of its value and significance, on the contrary. 'Enriched' by the misery of the century, distancing itself from it, contradicting it and confronting it, it was reasserted — in East and West, both in the form of a mantram for individuals and as a mantram for humanity as a whole.

★

'It would not be a correct judgement of the event of the Christmas Conference of 1923 to see it as an affair solely of importance to the members of the Society' — were the emphatic words of Zeylmans in 1956,[13] in which he pinpointed an important aspect also with regard to the meditation itself. A great deal can be said in support of the fact that the 'foundation' signified the concerns not only of the intimate circle of people around Rudolf Steiner, and not only the founding in Dornach itself, but potentially *every* individual of the modern age, who see themselves having to deal with the task of actively maintaining their humanity in the face of the challenges and catastrophes of the present and the future. It is by no means only the anthroposophists who will have to face these problems, on the contrary,[14] one can hear the words of the mantram 'sounding' in one's own heart, Rudolf Steiner said at the end of 1923. This process of 'hearing' the words of the Foundation Stone in one's own heart will probably acquire even more significance and reality in the future, and can be an enormous help to people — to every single one of those who open themselves to it — in particular, defined moments, or in the general course of life.

It is against this background that this small introductory book is being offered to assist in the spreading of the Foundation Stone meditation — of an understanding of its historic place in the catastrophic twentieth century, and the humanising contribution it could make to the future. The first pupils of Rudolf Steiner to have lived with the meditation have, for many years now, been in the spiritual world. They have taken with them their personal testimony of the value and quality that familiarising oneself with the mantram can have for both individuals and the community. The basic books and studies by Willem Zeylmans van Emmichoven and Sergei O. Prokofieff (as well as a few further anthroposophical writers)[15] are, however, available, and these open up deep layers of meditative treasures and how to use them, and are among the most significant works in the whole of the secondary category of anthroposophical literature. At the same time, we cannot dismiss the idea altogether that these works are too much for many people interested in principle, overtaxing them both from the point of view of quality as well as quantity, as the level at which anthroposophy is dealt with here exceeds their level of understanding, receptiveness and reading capacity. These works largely assume that a reader is already well acquainted with anthroposophy, this being a justified assumption, as the Foundation Stone meditation and the event of the Dornach Christmas Conference signified both an esoteric and an exoteric culmination of Rudolf Steiner's activity, a final intensification and a conclusion of the building up of anthroposophy, its foundations and its content, that had been proceeding without a break for more than three decades.

This situation regarding the reception of the meditation, however, involves a real dilemma, one in which the whole of anthroposophy and the anthroposophical movement to a certain extent find themselves at the beginning of the twenty-first century. People who know of anthroposophy and are its friends are aware of the importance of the various levels of this spiritual science, whereas many other people have almost no idea what it is, although a number of aspects of anthroposophy could signify an important help for their personal life, and also for their professional work in modern civilization. In view of the social challenge and the existing real spiritual 'peaks' of anthroposophy, we often find at present the tendency for members to stick together in small circles. A way is often chosen to make spiritual science popular by giving out a shallow version of it, a method that is seldom effective and is not good for the reputation of Rudolf Steiner's work and his person, and leads to very few positive results. No amount of propaganda avoids encountering the fact that one does not acquire anthroposophy free of charge and that it is not as easy to acquire as a lot of things on offer today; becoming inwardly involved with it is hard work. Part of the present problem, however, is that, on the other hand, it is by no means clear to innumerable contemporaries whether this effort to get the mantram across has any sense at all — and, if need be, *how* it could be done. The final result of this is that we have two groups of people, totally different both in size and in the sort of people they are: those who are knowledgeable, friends of the work of Rudolf Steiner, and the large numbers of others, outsiders and non-participants. Where the Foundation Stone meditation is concerned, and Rudolf Steiner published this himself (but only in the form of a localised newsletter connected with the weekly journal *Das Goetheanum*), the situation in which it now finds itself can certainly be called a tragic one. Although given originally in a very special connection, the meditation could signify a large and very likely unique support in the difficult times now and to come, by helping to provide people with a fresh impetus in creating a basis for a new beginning for their ego, and to restore again the image of man. It is the 'quintessence of the whole of anthroposophy' ('for its very essence is the human being')[16] and, as very little else does, it leads, as a meditation, directly to the being of man. It is at the same time both its beginning and its end, its Alpha and Omega. ('I am the Alpha and Omega, the beginning and the end' Revelations, 1:8.) In the words of Rudolf Grosse, 'the Foundation Stone meditation is the next step in human progress'[17] — by means of it, and in company with it, individual human beings and humanity as a whole can develop forces for the future. But, in actual fact, at present it lives on Earth, comparatively speaking, in only a few individuals.

In view of this situation this present study is offered as a contribution to help bring the Foundation Stone meditation afresh to people's notice in these dark times of our century and the near future. We should not get tired of 'regarding this meditation from ever further aspects', Sergei O. Prokofieff wrote in 1982.[18] In the changing conditions of the times it will reveal ever more to human beings, provided we really 'hear' it in our hearts. Humankind needs this mantram, and the whole of Rudolf Steiner's knowledge of man, in an age of persistent extremes in which progressive destruction of the Earth's living foundations and a violent distortion of the human image is being pursued, as though attempts are being made to change it into something else, right into the physical body — from stem cell research to molecular genetics and body technology.[19] It is obviously a justified question to ask what a meditative study is capable of achieving in the face of a complex of industrial forces working in this direction — and whether the Foundation Stone meditation as such is not much too complicated and difficult to give support to human beings in the form of the power to strengthen in themselves their own humanity.[20] On the other hand it seems worth considering that actually what holds the world together at its core — and does so still — is most probably of a spiritual nature; and that a secret of Steiner's effectiveness — and of *all* really Christian/esoteric activity — consists of making the deepest statements in a simple form in a way which (at least to a certain extent) can enter into the living space of *every* human being who is of good will. This would be a real way to prepare for the future. In 1907 Rudolf Steiner said in Munich: 'People who practise esoteric exercises grow spiritually into the future; they experience in themselves what will come about one day in the future, and what they experience in this way is what we know as the higher worlds. These represent future conditions of humankind.'[21]

I owe my personal thanks to Rudolf Steiner and Sergei O. Prokofieff that this book came about.

Peter Selg
Arlesheim and Brissage, Easter 2011

1.

'Evil Forces have taken strong hold of Humanity . . .'

The Destruction of the Twentieth Century

We confess — and perhaps we shall perish. But praise be — the Christ has become our brother. Our destiny is irreparable. For what power will deliver us from the mysterious seal of our belonging. Therefore: Where the world is concerned we are afraid. But in the world that has been overcome we are at peace. In the Christ World there is our peace. That is where it is.
Maria Krehbiel-Darmstädter, 13.8.1942.[22]

Maria Krehbiel-Darmstädter, January 1942

In the summer of 1942 Maria Krehbiel-Darmstädter (1892–1943), a German of Jewish descent aged 50, was living in the little French town of Limonest near Lyon, in the unoccupied part of France. In October 1940, together with nearly 2,000 other Jews, she was deported from Mannheim to the camp at Gurs, in the Pyrenees, where, under the most terrible conditions, she survived for 14 months. At the end of December 1941, because of a severe heart condition, she was released temporally from the camp, and, under police supervision, given leave to go and stay in a guesthouse in Limonest until her intended return to Gurs. Whilst she was in Limonest, Maria Krehbiel-Darmstädter remained closely connected with her fellow sufferers in the camp, people with whom she shared the same fate; she received a number of letters every day from the fateful place, and wrote to her friends there in continuation of the pastoral activity she had been engaged in in Gurs. During March and June, her sick leave residence period was extended twice. So she was still there at the beginning of August 1942, when the evacuating of the camp in Gurs began and all the prisoners were taken by train, in 'the final solution of the Jewish problem', to Auschwitz to be put to death in the gas chambers there.

Maria Krehbiel-Darmstädter still did not know the full details regarding these happenings at the time when, in the first week of August 1942, the daily letters bringing news from Gurs abruptly failed to appear, and all was silent. Yet she had bad premonitions in her own particular sensitive, clear-sighted way. On 9 August she wrote to her friend Margot Junod:

> It is extremely hard to *go on* living from day to day. And to erase the experiences of fear and sympathy, the readiness to escape to a condition of nothing-but-the-wish: for a long time they have exceeded the level of what can be imagined.
>
> Everyone is in a state of deep shock. And we are recoiling: from the present and from the future — and almost from the past. Nothing is keeping its shine or its meaning and character. None of the inner forces we had built up are capable of coping with the indescribable horror.
>
> And everything that existed before was only still a dream. — Even G[urs] was a bad dream compared to this reality of nightmare.

Maria Krehbiel-Darmstädter was an esoteric pupil of Rudolf Steiner's, and whilst in Gurs her conduct had been exemplary. Despite the diffi-cult condition in the camp she had maintained her inner life and com-

forted many of her fellow prisoners with her extraordinary composure
— confident mentally, yet modest, and this made a big impression in
the barracks and its surroundings. 'Tirelessly she dragged herself around
the camp with the aid of her wooden stick to help those people who
either bodily or mentally did not have the strength to stand up to life
by themselves any more.'[23] 'She was a really extraordinary person and
she helped a great many people there in their inner need. She herself
went through all the privations and foul treatment, apparently unaf-
fected by them, thinking only of others. She made a [...] powerful
spiritual impression.'[24] She was hesitant in accepting temporary 'leave
of absence' for she was not prepared to save her own life if her friends
and fellow sufferers had to remain in Gurs. Her consent to move to
Limonest was *only* made on the condition that she would return later
on to the camp, as well as in the knowledge that she would be able,
from Limonest, to help the prisoners by means of her letters, and also
be able to gather the strength for her future work at the camp. Whilst
in Gurs she had never complained, but had deployed all her capabilities
to extract the best out of the difficult situation and to help others. But
by the August of 1942, in view of the lack of news from her friends in
Gurs and the first suspicions of what was happening in the death camps
in Poland, her life in Limonest became daily more unbearable. On
August 18 she wrote to her brother:

> I am spending the most terrible and painful days here in front of my
> desk in an indescribable state of uncertainty. I have lost my con-
> nection with most of my friends in Gurs who have suddenly passed
> through a tremendous change in their lives, which has snatched
> them away from me.
>
> Maybe we shall meet again tomorrow, perhaps this is only a short
> separation, and writing will have proved unnecessary. —
>
> But at present I am clinging desperately to habits of years, and
> when no letters arrive with news, everything remains so empty and
> there is nothing to do for the rest of the day — except — : to wait for
> tomorrow and to *hope*: and this is a trial that sucks the heart dry —
>
> Of course one looks for something to do; you do a bit of
> mending, wash a few things, rummage around in your room — sift
> through books — think about what you would leave there, if —
> what you would do without — if it came to it — this is how you are
> preparing yourself, without really being able to achieve the real, the

big, the powerful state necessary for a decisive preparation, that would mean an acceptance of what has to happen.

This is how you weaken yourself through your own weakness! A breakthrough to a dedicated acceptance of an unknown departure (on the other hand only a passage to a further level of suffering, meaning to a level of knowledge) is not succeeding: Not yet.

At the end of the letter she added (as an afterthought):

We are the kind of creatures who are in need of redemption.
Instead, we are shown further burdens; and having already been put to the test with other ones, they are sharpening our compassion, until it at last almost *is* a redeeming experience to be able, oneself, to enter into the state of the sort of suffering that is genuine, for one has prepared it for oneself.

Maria Krehbiel-Darmstädter had never been afraid of her own dying and death. The transition into the world of the spirit, into the sphere of the 'heavens' that she understood to be her own real home, was close to her heart, despite her love for the Earth. 'In Christ we die' was a truth that gave her full confidence. However, the 'nightmare' that took place in August 1942, and that she experienced in her own feeling from a distance, was a bad dream compared to this *reality of a nightmare*, and there was the murder of her fellow human beings, her sisters and brothers, in inconceivable cruelty — in the industrial gas chambers of Auschwitz by means of 'Zyklon B', beyond the range of any humane death, in the demonic attempt to achieve complete destruction of the ego. 'Nothing keeps its shine and its sense and shape. None of the inner forces we had built up are capable of coping with this indescribable horror.' To approach death in this way *was* something she was afraid of; she was afraid for her friends, and finally for herself, too. In Limonest she expected to be deported any day, and found herself in a hopeless position. With severe heart disease and suffering from disturbances of the rhythmic system, she lived in a state of the greatest stress, under increasing pressure, concerned not only for herself, but for the whole situation of the victims of persecution. In January 1942 the decision was taken at the Wannsee meeting in Berlin to murder eleven million Jews. So, there was the incessant running of trains taking the imprisoned people to Auschwitz and to other death camps. To another friend who had already been given temporary leave from the camp at Gurs, Maria Krehbiel-Darmstädter wrote, on 21 August 1942, of her fear, and the occurrence of breathlessness that *'forgets that God has laid his name in every soul'*. She then, however, continued in a more positive direction by saying:

> We therefore could have had nothing else to do then than — breathe. In and out. When facing danger this last remaining rhythm supplies the answer to everything. 'Practise spirit presence in soul equilibrium — where the weaving deeds of universal becoming unite the individual I with the I of the World, and you will truly feel in the active life of your soul. For the Christ Will is present all around in World rhythms shedding grace on our souls. Spirits of Light, may what is formed by the West have been quickened by the light of the East, proclaiming: In Christ death becomes life . . .' What joy to be able to escape to the calm reliance of such wisdom — breathing, observing. Receiving assurance right into one's soul.

The person who received the letter, Toni Schwarz, who belonged to the Freiburg Christian Community under Friedrich Doldinger, very likely knew to which words of wisdom Maria Krehbiel-Darmstädter had turned for her refuge in her need, and where she had again found 'soul assurance'. The lines she quotes are part of the second verse of Rudolf Steiner's Foundation Stone meditation: 'In times of danger this last remaining rhythm is the answer to everything.'

In the late summer and autumn of 1942, Maria Krehbiel-Darmstädter was restored to her former inner strength, though she was heavily attacked and bullied. She was eventually arrested in December 1942, and in February 1943 was taken from the transit camp Drancy to Auschwitz, where she very probably died in the gas chamber on the day of her arrival. Her last written communication was on 5 February 1943 from Drancy, in which she expressed the feeling of becoming weaker both in body and in mind; in the end, her last words were Paul's words in his letter to the Hebrews (13:14): 'We have no peace here. But we are looking to a future one'.

How Maria Krehbiel-Darmstädter felt in her innermost being in the last weeks, days and hours before her death is not known. On 20 January 1943 she had written and told Margot Junod that she was gathering herself together 'in an almost continuous prayer'. In Drancy, the Polish Jews with whom she was detained and were awaiting transport to Auschwitz, called her 'mère Maria'. She very likely was helping other people in need right to the end, even while she could hardly manage herself any more. The journey in wintertime, of several days duration, to the Polish concentration and death camp, in overcrowded cattle trucks, with almost no air, water and food, was already a martyrdom. On 13 February, together with 997 Jewish fellow prisoners, Maria Krehbiel-Darmstädter arrived at the entrance to Auschwitz–Birkenau. She was bewildered by the long journey, by being driven out of the trucks, by the presence of the loud and brutal S.S. men, the sight of the innumerable barracks, and the wretched cold of upper Silesia, as well as the smoke and the smell of the crematoria that filled the whole place. Her last steps she took on Earth were — after being dragged over the site — down the steps to the gas chamber.

Viktor Frankl, who had also been in Auschwitz — even if only for a short time — and who survived life in the camps at Theresienstadt, Kaufering and Türkheim, wrote afterwards: 'Humans are the beings who invented gas chambers, but at the same time they are also the beings who have entered the gas chambers, walking upright, with a prayer on their lips'.[25] Maria Krehbiel-Darmstädter is very likely to have been one of those people who entered the gas chamber walking upright with a 'prayer on her lips'. She knew a great many prayers and meditations, and held them in her heart — among them the Foundation Stone meditation of Rudolf Steiner's. 'In times of danger this one remaining rhythm is the answer to everything.'

★

Elie Wiesel, who in his youth was detained for nine months in Auschwitz with his father, and lost both his mother and his little sister there, stressed that in Auschwitz not only did one and a half million people die a violent death, but that the 'idea of a human being' was also murdered there.[26]

It was of this 'idea of a human being' that Rudolf Steiner's meditation spoke — and when in December 1923, on the occasion of the Christmas Conference of the General Anthroposophical Society, he gave it to his anthroposophical friends, it was done in the knowledge of the difficult path his Dornach listeners and friends would have to follow in the twentieth century. Rudolf Steiner had not only experienced the First World War but also the disastrous middle European developments after the end of the dreadful killings — the harsh peace treaty of Versailles, which the forces of nationalism directly called a making of a peace treaty given in revenge, the political radicalising and brutalising, the growing anti-semitism and militarising, but also the totalitarianism and dictatorial developments in Russia under Lenin, Trotsky and Stalin. In the spring of 1920 a book appeared by Karl Binding and Alfred Hoche about 'the vindication of the extermination of lives not worth living', a book fraught with consequences, and which prepared the way for euthanasia in the age when Darwinism became a social reality. In the same year in December, in Dornach, Rudolf Steiner had given a warning of a further world war ('People are preparing themselves for the next great world war. Culture will be even further destroyed'),[27] and he had spoken of an increasing 'love of evil' on the part of human beings.

Evil forces, a love of evil has taken strong hold of humankind.[28]

In Dornach, on Easter Saturday 1920, he had said with regard to the situation in middle Europe:

> These two things are looming for the entire Christian element of the nineteenth and twentieth century: nationalism, the luciferic form of anti-Christianity, and that which is culminating in Leninism, Trotskyism, the ahrimanic form of anti-Christianity. These are the spades with which, in the present time, the grave of Christianity is to be dug, and people who have insight will feel that a mood is prevailing in those areas similar to the actual mood of Easter Saturday.
>
> The bringer of Christianity lies in his grave, and people are placing a stone on it. People have put two stones upon the representative of Christianity; nationalism and superficial social customs.[29]

Ten weeks before the Christmas Conference and the handing over of the Foundation Stone meditation, Rudolf Steiner was approached on 13 October 1923 by one of the young guards at the Goetheanum, Georg Groot. A few days before this Groot had heard Steiner speaking in one of the lectures to workmen in Dornach about the serious consequences of lethal cyanide poisoning on human beings in their after death existence, and asked him to say more about it. Steiner told him more about what had been in the lecture[30] and Groot gives us the following report:

> To my question as to whether in a subsequent war hydrocyanic gasses would be used Rudolf Steiner said 'no', but that further fearful things were in preparation. To my question as to whether that would be in America, he said 'no, in Germany!'[31]

What Rudolf Steiner was referring to in this remark is not clear. Hydrocyanic gas Zyklon B did not after all come into use on the battlefield during World War Two but in the Nazi concentration death camps that were set up and became big business during the war. That was the poison used to murder over 5 million Jews, but also innumerable members of the Sinti and Roma, resistance fighters, political prisoners and socially 'undesirable' people, including thousands of patients. Many more weapons of death and destruction were invented and developed beyond these by the German National Socialists and the scientists associated with them. Since the attack on Poland in September 1939, German physicists worked at the 'Uranverein', an office sponsored by the army's weapons' industry, at constructing an atom bomb that just escaped being put to use.

★

Rudolf Steiner heard about the attempted Munich coup of Hitler's and Ludendorff's in November 1923, just six weeks before the Christmas Conference in Dornach. Rudolf Steiner spoke about the fact that after the take-over of power he would not be able to enter German territory any more,[32] and that a Nazi regime would bring 'tremendous devastation to middle Europe'.[33] Rudolf Steiner, who as early as 1921 had already been sharply attacked by Hitler in a magazine article as a 'gnostic and anthroposophist',[34] arranged for his Berlin home in Motz Street to be closed down and all the book stocks of the Philosophisch-Anthro-posophischer Verlag (publisher) there to be sent to Dornach in neutral Switzerland. During the night of 8/9 November 1923, the night of the Munich coup, his colleague Anna Samweber — a former Communist and a sober, pragmatic woman — had (on her rounds as a guard at the Goetheanum) had a waking vision of Berlin going up in flames. Consequently she petitioned her teacher for something to keep her spirits up in the days to come ('anthroposophy is a goblet from which we can refresh ourselves ever and again when even worse times come, and we no longer have you, Herr Doctor; can you give us some words to keep us going?'). Anna Samweber received this help from Rudolf Steiner soon afterwards in the form of a mantric meditation:

To my Berlin Friends

Human beings look
With eyes produced by this world;
What they look at connects them
To world joy and world pain,
Connects them with everything

That comes into being here, but no less
To everything that is plunging down
into dark realms of the abyss.

Human beings see
With eyes given them by the spirit;
What they see connects them
To spiritual hope and spiritual endurance;
It connects them to everything
That is rooted in eternity
And which bears fruit for ever.

But human beings can see
Only if they themselves feel their inner eye
To be a spiritual part of God
Which, in the temple of the human body
On the stage of the soul,
Carries out deed of the Gods.

Humankind is in forgetfulness
of the inner forces, the forces of God.
But we want to bring them
Into the bright light of consciousness,
And hold in our hearts, above the rubble and ashes,
the flame of the Gods.

Even if lightning were to smash
Our bodily covering to pieces
We would erect soul coverings
Out of a knowing that is as delicate as light, as firm as steel.
The falling away of the outer layers
Shall become the arising
of the innermost soul.
Suffering forces itself on us
Out of overpowering forces of matter;
Hope rays out
Even when darkness is swirling around us;
And in time to come, it will stream into our memory
If, after the darkness
We may live again in the light.
We do not want it to happen

That this beam of light will be lacking
In future brightness
Because in our present suffering
We have not planted it in our souls.

Anna Samweber's parting from Rudolf Steiner, whom she had lived close
to for many years, and whom she would never see again, was very warm
and moving: 'Rudolf Steiner was very serious. He was standing (in his
studio) in front of the statue of Christ. The words he had for me were
lying on the table. As he handed me the sheet of paper he said: Well, Sam,
these lines contain a lot of sadness, you know; but the time will come
when all of you will read the greatest sadness between the lines. He put his
hands on my heart, and continued: tell our Berlin friends . . . I shall then
be with you'.[35]

After this meeting, in the barely one and a quarter years remaining to
Rudolf Steiner for the continuation of his work, he did not come to
Berlin again — the lecture planned there for October 1924 had to be
cancelled due to illness. His words, but his picture as well, accompanied
Anna Samweber and the 'Berlin friends' of the Anthroposophical Society
during the bomb damage that cost more than 20,000 human lives and
culminated in the air attack of 30 March 1945, on the day that was exactly
20 years after Rudolf Steiner left the Earth. Anna Samweber continued
living at 17 Motz Street in Berlin, the home of Steiner's Berlin activities
and the geographical starting place of the anthroposophical movement.
The row of houses opposite and much besides, in Hitler's 'Führer' town,
the spot where the Wannsee Conference and all his war strategy took
place, was completely destroyed. However, Anna Samweber and the
'Berlin friends' went on working after 1945 and setting up many
anthroposophical initiatives afresh — 'The flame of the Gods in human
hearts'.

★

On the occasion of the Dornach Christmas Conference, which occurred
soon after the conversation with Georg Groot and Anna Samweber,
Rudolf Steiner endeavoured to found the anthroposophical worldwide
Society anew, and to call into being an anthroposophically active initiative, with the School of Spiritual Science in Dornach as its source.[36] All
the events, new developments and future projects set going at this conference — and which must be seen in connection with the background of

what was Europe's threatening plunge 'into the dark depths of the abyss', signifying the transposing or extension of the materialistic thoughts of death of the past century[37] — was clearly visible in the beginning of the 1920s:

> When we look out at the world today we have, for years, been presented with a tremendous amount of things to do with destruction. Forces are at work, which give us a strong presentiment of the sort of depths Western civilization may be steering towards. (Rudolf Steiner, 1.1.1924)[38]

Rudolf Steiner gave the meditation of the Foundation Stone verses into the hands of the members of the General Anthroposophical Society; the foundation of the Society was not meant to be laid in Dornach soil but in everyone's hearts. This was where the future work for the Earth, for individual people, for all mankind, was meant to come from. Rudolf Steiner, in consequence, both wanted to and had to work with great intensity at the School of Spiritual Science in Dornach, with its faculties or 'sections', to introduce humanistic medicine, to bring understanding and therapy (and not euthanasia) to so-called 'retarded' children (which Rudolf Steiner called children in need of special care), to establish new pedagogy for helping children to be more human (an education towards freedom), and to treat the Earth in a living way (instead of offering it industrialised and commercialised 'agri-technology'), and to bring many more peace initiatives into the world, which would have at their centre a real image and understanding of the human being. What would have to be at the very core of all the active work of the future would have to be the recognising of the form, the being of man, in every person, and also the realising of this in oneself. Rudolf Steiner said farewell to the members of the Anthroposophical Society, at the end of the conference, in the following words:[39]

'My dear friends, as you leave here, take with you your warm hearts in which you have planted the foundation stone of the Anthroposophical Society; take these warm hearts with you *so that you can be therapeutically active in the world.*' Rudolf Steiner was well aware that his colleagues would have difficult paths ahead of them, withstanding and opposing the predominating 'spirit of the times', even to the point of hardship and persecution. Right until his sickbed claimed him at the end of September 1924 (nine months after the Christmas Conference), he did everything in his power to help them by holding special courses for anthroposophicallyorientated doctors, educational therapists, teachers, priests and farmers, and visited new ventures in an advisory capacity. The middle European world, in which the various initiatives were starting up, was likely to become more and more complicated, as Rudolf Steiner already emphasised, not only when giving the course on biodynamic agriculture in Silesian Koberwitz, near Breslau (in the district of what was to be the later 'General Gouvernement'). In a lecture in June 1924 he spoke about 'middle Europe's terrible destiny' and its possible collapse,[40] and when asked he said more about this in Graf Keyserlingk's house. 'Europe is sitting on a volcano, but has not noticed it', he said out of deep concern for the future of our war-torn civilization. If one were able to take part in the table conversations between the courses you would have heard Rudolf Steiner referring to the storms that were about to rage through the world again, as though they were inevitable. He spoke of the destruction of Middle European cities (Rudolf Meyer).[41]

Four months before the beginning of the Agricultural Course, on 8 February 1924, the first human was killed by the use of gas, in a cell in a state prison of Nevada — the 'fastest and most humane method of killing a person', said the Major responsible.[42] Not a few of Steiner's followers were of Jewish extraction, and lost their lives in this way two decades later in the Nazi death camps — among them Maria Krehbiel-Darmstädter.

★

The twentieth century was indeed an age of destruction — marked and stamped by the gigantic wars and their consequences. In the twentieth century more people perished — were ordered or allowed to be killed — than ever before in the total history of mankind. 'A new estimation of the "mega deaths" of the century amount to 187 million, corresponding to more than one in ten of the whole of the world population of 1900' (Hobsbawm).[43] Never before in the history of mankind had it been possible to have such wars as we had in the twentieth century, in an industrial/technological dimension that released unimaginable forces of destruction; and, whether targeted or not, hit the mark. The development of highly technical air warfare and the bombing of cities in World War Two introduced the 'carpet bombing massacre' of the civilian population — and both the world wars were of a *total* nature, including all the weaponry, all the industrial, economic and propaganda resources, which drew in everyone capable of being active, amassing a previously unknown dynamic. This — as well as the assessment resulting in the second half of the twentieth century, were typified by a 'growing brutality and inhumanity' of the twentieth century (Hobsbawm)[44] and stretched from the first application of poison gas (which the German armed forces began using in 1915) to the application of the atom bombs at Hiroshima and Nagasaki. The occurring scenarios of mass destruction became more apocalyptic, and the new impersonal way of running a war, which 'reduced killing or mutilating to one performance restricting it to the pressing of a key or the moving of a lever',[45] and making it possible for cascades of destruction to take place without any conscientious awareness. In the last decades of the twentieth century the scenarios of destruction, of the massacring, the cruelty, the ghastly torture, which the century developed and carried further in its own terrible way, appeared every-where for the first time in the form of films and 'games', and entered in this way into the virtual spheres of the lives and daily experience of children and young people. People running amok, and even would-be assassins and suicide bombers appeared in increasing numbers and effectiveness. 'Evil forces, a love of evil, have strongly possessed humanity'. (Rudolf Steiner)

In the wake of the devastating wars, the twentieth century brought unimaginable forced expulsions and the attempt to murder whole nations, beginning with the genocide of the Christian Armenians by the Turks (who had a coalition with Germany), carried out during World War One and which claimed about 1.5 million victims. Then came the attempted 'extermination' of 11 million Jews by the Nazis at the begin-ning of the 40s, half of which was achieved, roughly 5 million Jewish victims dying in the concentration and death camps of the 'Third Reich'. New words found their way into the world language of the twentieth century — not, however, of the kind hoped for and intended by Rudolf Steiner, namely the concept 'unbornness' (to describe the pre-conceptual state of existence of human individualities)[46] — but, among others, the word 'genocide'.

With such violent changes as these the structure of earthly life, the form of civilization and social life as they had been up till now, went almost to pieces — even if this did not happen everywhere at the same time, or was directly visible. Already during World War One, millions of people had taken flight and by May 1945, at the end of World War Two, in Europe alone there were about 4.5 million people uprooted. But this by no means spells the end of all the chaos; on the contrary, murder, torture and mass expulsion determined everyday life in the second half of the twentieth century too, even if this was in other parts of the world. National collapse and dissolution, focal points of unrest, 'bloodbath zones' and horrific acts of violence by powermongers who had close connections of interest with leading world rulers, followed at ever shorter intervals, and as a result of the ever-increasing scope of the privatisation of weapons of destruction had the power to spread their destructive force over the whole Earth. Already, in 1993, the blowing up of the World Trade Centre in New York was attempted for the first time, and Hobsbawm wrote:

> [...] The century ended with worldwide unrest, the nature of which was unclear, and there are no mechanisms at our disposal to end it or to keep it under control.[47]

The gap between the rich and poor countries widened in the twentieth century to an enormous extent — combined with a tremendous 'population explosion' in the developing countries, which set the form for the middle of the century, and will similarly shape the future of planet Earth.

From a scientific, technological point of view Europe remained, despite the two world wars that were kindled here, a significant factor. But the dominant role it had held up till 1914 did not apply any longer. In the first half of the twentieth century it had become a 'dark continent'[48] from which sprung the 'totalitarian' age affecting the whole Earth, in a complete distortion and reversal of those positions of value and perspective which middle Europe had previously held — the age of the development of consciousness in modern times. In Germany there arose fascism of the Nazi type, and in Russia the dictatorship of Marxism–Leninism, which brought with them indescribable misery and destruction. Both of these ideologies, when compared with one another, have, despite superficial differences, much in common[49] — including the complete submission of people to the State, with the intention of destroying both individualism and culture, as well as aiming to destroy any form of individual or social future. They promised lasting solutions for a world torn by crises but were themselves the producers, the expression and the result of the crises, and the abyss.

This was the way — directly and indirectly — in which a lot of things came to an end in the twentieth century, which previous to this had lasted for hundreds and thousands of years. Regarding the worldwide changes in social connections in the course of the 'short' twentieth century, Hobsbawm wrote:

The [. . .] in many respects most bewildering transformation was the dissolving of the old social and connecting structures and, hand in hand with this, the bursting apart of the connecting links between the generations: that is, between the past and the present. This came particularly clearly to light in the most advanced states of western capitalism, where both state and private ideologies became increasingly dominated by the values of an absolutely asocial individualism, although it frequently happened that the very people who implemented this themselves complained about the social consequences. But this tendency occurred in other places too, and was encouraged not only by the erosion of traditional societies and religion, but also by the destruction, or self-destruction, of the societies in which 'socialism actually existed'.[50]

At the end of the twentieth century Eric Hobsbawm and other historians and socialists described the structural tremors in the balance of the whole of planet Earth, which was an intrinsic part of the closing century. Among these there were the greatest ecological crises the Earth's organism had ever shown, and the result of the desire for profit on the part of business enterprise, as well as the technological interventions and ways of proceeding, which wanted to increase ever further the 'living standard' of the inhabitants of the richest industrial nations at the cost of the whole biosphere. Millions of scientists worked at the end of the twentieth century at natural-scientific research, experimental development and industrial/technological transplanting, but only a disappearing minority of them are looking into the forces and laws of the living world with regard to their protection and preservation.

All in all, the destruction left behind from the twentieth century concerns all areas of earthly existence — beginning with the violated physical/etheric equilibrium of the Earth's landscapes, elemental forces and beings, which have partly succumbed to irrevocable extinction or have entered the 'alliance with Ahriman' prophesied by Steiner).[51] Proceeding to the realm Rudolf Steiner called 'astrality', innumerable animals and animal species died out or are in a state of decline because, due to the changed and damaged Earth, they can no longer find suitable living conditions. By comparison the 'astral' soul forces of human beings went through a process of weakening and alienation; they lost not only their metaphysical attachment but the unity of the ego set above them, which as such became prey to an increasing instability. By means of this whole process it became possible for forces working through politics and ideologies to affect various individual soul forces for their own purposes, and in the twentieth century this was happening in a fundamental way. And not least, the conditions towards which Hobsbawm had drawn our attention — 'the dissolving of the old social and connecting structures' and 'the bursting apart of the connecting links between the generations, between past and present' — led to a loss of cultural as well as individual memory, both of history and of personal recollections, which weakened the sustainability of both individuals and communities, and prepared the ground for almost unlimited destruction and processes of violence. At the end of the twentieth century Sergei O. Prokofieff gave a most convincing description of the way death forces ruled supreme, in the following words: 'The death forces have gained mastery in most of the areas of present civilization and are gradually driving it to perdition'.[52] And the philosopher Isaiah Berlin, although he also knew the present age from numerous positive sides, described the twentieth century as 'the most terrible century in the history of the West'.[53] The Jewish violinist Yehudi Menuhin wrote:

> If I wanted to sum up the twentieth century I would say that it produced the greatest hopes that humankind has ever had, *and it shattered all our illusions and all our ideals*.'[54]

In his summing up account in *The Age of Extremes* Eric Hobsbawm sketched the situation at the end of the twentieth century in the following words:

> We know that behind the impenetrable cloud of the ignorance and uncertainty about details the historical forces that have shaped this century are continuing to work. We live in a world that has been hijacked, turned upside down and uprooted by gigantic economic and technical/scientific processes connected to the development of capitalism that have been the dominating force in the last two to three centuries. We know, or reasonably assume that this cannot continue ad infinitum. The future cannot be a continuation of the past. There are not only outer but, as it were, inner signs showing us that we have come to a point of a historic crisis. The forces that have released our technical/scientific economy have in the meantime become strong enough to be able to destroy the environment, i.e. the actual foundation of all human life. And the structures of human

societies themselves, including even some of the social foundations
of the capitalist economy, are about to be destroyed due to the
erosion of what has been inherited from our human past. Our world
risks both explosion or implosion. It has to change. We do not know
where we are going.[55]

It is not difficult to show in detail the way in which Rudolf Steiner's life
work unfolded in contrast to these forces of decline, and to see and
understand them as a fundamental counter gesture; not, however, in the
context of that absurd, selective, grand 'esotericism' that his biographers
— in particular Helmut Zander — accused him of, at the beginning of the
twentieth century. The Foundation Stone, too, represents a humanised
new beginning, from out of the forces of resistance of the developed
human I — with its social connections and its love for the Creation, its
qualities and beings. Rudolf Steiner knew that real remedial action, the
stopping and reversing of the whole destructive process affecting civilization, can only be achieved on a grand scale — by working out and
applying a different concept of science, different social structures, values
and aims, both in an individual and in a communal respect. His whole
life's work was aimed towards this, as was also his intention regarding the
work of the School of Spiritual Science in Dornach. On its own, the
Foundation Stone meditation could do little or nothing — it was and is, at
one and the same time, the mantric basis of the whole of the School's and
of the future set-up in Dornach — a real community achievement, which
is meant to come into being out of the forces of awakened egos, their
initiatives, their consciousness and their abilities in the social realm. The
human ego is of decisive importance for all future matters. As Sergei O.
Prokofieff says: 'It is not so difficult to conceive of the fact that today the
human "I" is at the very centre of all human and world problems. All the
catastrophic wars and crises taking place in the world today are, in the last
resort, only the outer expression of the inner battles of us human beings,
and their scene of action is in our hearts.'[56] The existential problems of the
world, and also their possible solution and healing, originate in human
egos and nowhere else.

Even if all that Rudolf Steiner had planned to do in, and with the help
of, Dornach up till 30 March 1925 and beyond could not be adequately
implemented — and in academic circles and political commentating his
anthroposophy first and foremost received hatred, mockery and malice
(and Steiner's biographic critics at the beginning of the twenty-first

century continued in exactly the same strain) — there were many individuals who went out into the world with the Foundation Stone meditation, among them Maria Krehbiel-Darmstädter, who took it in her heart into Auschwitz and into the realm of total destruction. We can ask ourselves whether this mantram given by Steiner did not in Auschwitz spiritually resist and withstand 'the massacring' of the human image described by Wiesel — and already by the end of 1923 Rudolf Steiner had *also* formulated the intention to counter the coming destruction and dissolution, distortions and cancellations by opposing them with *the truth about man*, the concrete re-erecting of man's image and being. 'Everything is suffering shock. And we are recoiling. From the present and from the future — and almost from the past. Nothing is keeping its shine or its meaning and character. None of the inner forces we had built up are capable of coping with the 'unspeakable event', is what Maria Krehbiel-Darmstädter wrote in that disastrous summer of 1942 regarding the envisaged death camp and the demonic methods of death of the Nazis. But with the help of the Foundation Stone meditation she found her inner calm in Auschwitz. The mantric words have an up-building, beneficial and therapeutic effect, as has been experienced in the twentieth century by Rudolf Steiner's esoteric pupils in numerous ways in the realms of education, therapeutic education, medicine and personal life. 'In times of danger this unique rhythm is the answer to everything.'

After World War Two was over, Willem Zeylmans van Emmichoven eventually, through lecturing and holding seminars, brought the Foundation Stone meditation out into the world — he travelled through all the continents talking about it, about Rudolf Steiner and anthroposophy.[57] Zeylmans saw in the Foundation Stone meditation the foundation of every kind of future human and social interaction; in fact he saw it as the restoring archetypal image of a new world order out of the forces of the I that have reached out to include the whole of humanity. The book Zeylmans wrote about the Foundation Stone, which he published in 1956, thirteen years after the death of Maria Krehbiel-Darmstädter, he concluded with some thoughts about 'the new Isis' and about the future image of man. He ended with the words:

> The way in which Man will one day appear as bearer of the World Ego can only be dimly apprehended today. Nevertheless, further development of the forces of the soul will permit us, in due course, to behold the perfected figure of Man with the eye of the spirit.[58]

Erst erahnen lässt sich heute, wie der Mensch einst als Träger des Welten Ich in Erscheinung treten wird; doch eine Weiterentwicklung der Seelenkräfte wird nur zur gegebenen Zeit das vollendete Menschenbild mit Geistesaugen schauen lassen.[59]

2.

'In times of danger this unique rhythm is the answer to everything . . .'

The Foundation Stone Meditation

Those are the words of the Christ that are being addressed today out of the spiritual realms by a choir of divine spiritual hierarchies to every 'human soul' of present times.
Sergei O. Prokofieff.[60]

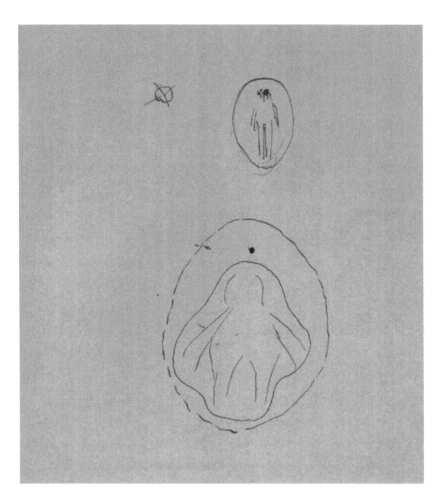

Illustration 2: A drawing of Rudolf Steiner's from The Notebooks of Rudolf Steiner, *edited by Etsuko Watari and Walter Kugler, Tokyo 2001, p. 17*

Human soul!
You live in the limbs
Which bear you through the world of space
In the flowing ocean of the spirit.
Practise *spirit-recognition*
In depths of soul,
Where in the wielding will
Of world creation
The individual I
Comes to being
In the I of God;
And you will truly *live*
In your body's cosmic being.

For the Father Spirit of the heights is present
In world depths begetting existence:
Spirits of Strength!
May there ring forth from the heights
The call re-echoed in the depths;
Proclaiming:
Humankind is born of God.
The elemental spirits hear it
In east, west, north, south:
*May hu*man beings *hear* it!

Human soul!
You live in the beat of heart and lung
Which leads you through the rhythm of time
Into the realm of your own soul's feeling.
Practise *spirit presence*
In soul composure,
Where the weaving deeds
Of universal becoming
Unite
The individual I
With the I of the world;
And you will truly *feel*
In the active life of your soul.

For the Christ Will is present all around
In world rhythms shedding grace on our souls;
Spirits of Light!
May what is formed by the west
Have been quickened in the light of the east;
Proclaiming:
In Christ death becomes life.
The elemental spirits hear it
In east, west, north, south:
*May hu*man beings *hear* it!

Human soul!
You live in the stillness of the head
Which from the founts of eternity
Disclose for you cosmic thoughts.
Practise *spirit beholding*
In thought calm,
Where the eternal aims of Gods
Give the light of spirit worlds
To the individual I
For will in freedom.
And you will truly *think*
In the founts of your human spirit.

For the spirit's cosmic thoughts are present
In world existence begging for light;
Spirits of Soul!
May there ascend from the depths
The plea heard in the heights;
Proclaiming:
In the spirit's cosmic thoughts the soul will
Awaken.
The elemental spirits hear it
In east, west, north, south:
*May hu*man beings *hear* it!

At the turning of time
Cosmic Spirit Light descended
Into the earthly stream of being;
Darkness of night

Had run its course;
The light of day
Shone forth in human souls:
Light
That gives warmth
To poor shepherds' hearts,
Light
That enlightens
The wise heads of kings.
God-given light.
Christ Sun,
Give warmth
To our hearts;
Give light
To our heads;
That what we found
From our hearts
What we guide
From our heads
Will be good.[61]

The first three verses of the Foundation Stone meditation begin with the call to man, or more exactly to the 'human soul', in its living reality, its actual existence on Earth, which, at the end of the nineteenth century and the beginning of the twentieth century was, from the direction of methodical materialism, constantly being disputed and denied. This call to the human soul, however, was not referring to a condition of rest, of merely being available or ready, but is a summons to continue developing — in spite of world conditions that are not helpful to soul/spiritual progress — which is absolutely demanded in the course of our further evolution, in the intensification and strengthening of our inner forces. As Rudolf Steiner repeatedly emphasised, since the twentieth century there has been the possibility that human beings, under the dominance of materialism and its apparent postulates of freedom, will lose their soul/spiritual autonomy in every realm of life, if they do not aim to make headway at promoting and acquiring the soul's own forces. At an end-of-year school conference of the teachers of the Stuttgart Waldorf School, Rudolf Steiner said that a situation could arise in which materialism would prove true:

> Then it could no longer be untrue to say 'the brain thinks' for it could be correct. By being entrenched in materialism there will not only be people being conceived who think wrongly about the body, the soul and the spirit, but people will actually be being conceived who *think* in a material way, *feel* in a material way. This means that materialism turns people into thinking automatons, and that human beings will become such that they think, feel and act as physical beings. And the task of anthroposophy is not merely to put correct world concepts in the place of wrong ones — that would be a theoretical request. The essence of anthroposophy today is not that the brain is to have other ideas, but to put other deeds into practice: to tear the spiritual/soul element out of the bodily/physical again, to raise their human nature into the realm of the soul/spiritual, so that they are not automatons in their thinking, feeling and sensations. Humanity today is in danger [...] of losing its soul/spiritual forces. We live at a time in which human beings are in danger of losing their souls to materialism. This is a serious matter. We have to face this fact.[62]

The call to the human soul, appealing to it to 'raise itself into the sphere of the soul and spirit' to that of self-awareness and self-development, leads in the course of the meditation to a clear understanding of its nature, of its own being and its connections. The human soul has connections with the body but also with the spirit; it is a central and mediating part of us and as such it enables us to have an earthly biography, which is a force of life lived by a spiritual individuality in space and time. ('The soul is actually the part of us through which we belong to our earthly biography.')[63] It is our soul forces that enable our spirit to form connections on Earth and go through a biographical process: it is by *thinking, feeling* and *will* that the soul lives in the earthly sphere — it is by means of these three forces that our individuality forms its earthly path. This is the manner in which it mediates between the past, the present and the future of the individual, also between the past of our pre-birth existence and our life after death, in that it enables our spirit to live in the *now* of earthly existence. In his book *Theosophy* Rudolf Steiner wrote:

> It [the soul] is what preserves present happenings in our memory. It snatches it from the past and takes it into spiritual duration. It also stamps these lasting experiences into the transitory nature of time, in that it does not spend its forces solely on passing pleasures but determines things itself and embodies its being in the actions it carries out. By means of memory our soul preserves our yesterdays; by means of action it prepares our tomorrows.[64]

However, our soul's thinking, as well as our feeling and willing, are all at the present time under threat; they have to find themselves, find their 'real' nature, so as not to pass through the serious consequences of a successive self-alienation and final annihilation ('Humanity is in danger today [. . .] of losing its soul and spirit'). As the meditation clearly points out it is 'real' thinking, feeling and will only that will lead to the future — it is solely through acquiring awareness of our soul forces and increasing their strength that the human soul will maintain its connections to the Earth, to other people and to the cosmos, and develop them further.

★

Human soul!
You live in the limbs
Which bear you through the world of space
In the flowing ocean of the spirit:
Practise *spirit-recognition*
In depths of soul,

Where in the wielding will
Of world creating
The individual I
Comes to being
In the I of God;
And you will truly *live*
In your body's cosmic being.

The first and basic direction in which the human soul orientates itself on Earth, both in the course of physiological development and also in the sphere of the Foundation Stone meditation, applies to our bodily limbs. We learn during our first year of earthly life to raise ourselves up; we acquire an upright position in earthly space, and we become increasingly able to guide our steps in the direction in which we want to go. What sets our limbs in motion is not the co-ordinating function and capacities that take place but our 'human soul' that *lives in reality* in the 'limbs', both when we are children and when we are grown-up.

Where our earthly will is concerned we move towards something other than ourselves; we are 'among the things outside', therefore beyond the limits of our own body, its inner space and its boundary. In deciding to do something and doing it, as Rudolf Steiner wrote in 1917 in his book *Riddles of the Soul*, 'we reach out beyond our body'. In the process of moving we are physically not dealing with anything the nature of which lies within our organism, but with an effect our organism has on the relationship of balance and of forces, existing between our organism and the outer world. Within our organism our will deals solely with the process of metabolism; but what happens as a result of this process is at the same time an essential part of the relationship of balance and the forces of the outer world; and the soul, by actively applying this will power, reaches beyond the field of the organism and actively takes part in what is going on in the outer world.[65] People who have the will to be active are 'in the flowing ocean of the spirit', i.e. in the spiritual structure of the environment, in the region of their concrete goals. They live in and with the things that are outside them, 'and take part in what is going on in the world outside'. They are with the other people and things they have gone to join. At the same time, without doubt, 'the flowing ocean of the spirit' also describes the sphere of our after-death existence. 'Human soul! You live in the limbs that bear you through the world of space *into the flowing ocean of the spirit*', was how Rudolf Steiner formulated it verbally during the Christmas Conference.[66] It is with the help of our legs that we walk through our earthly biography, the 'space world'. We make our way to our respective goals and do this until the moment when we come to a complete stop, and to the sort of rest that death signifies and brings us. At death our life's *path* is finished, and until this point is reached human beings encounter, in earthly *space* — by virtue of their legs — the forms of their destiny that belong to their existence; with the help of their limbs they meet the people, the places and the tasks that are theirs, and with which they make an active connection, both suffering karma and forming it anew. Then, when their life's path is concluded, their whole organization passes through a complete change.

And yet what appears at death is only the end of a process of dying that is an inherent part of our life's path and our physiology[67] — and not least in the area of the metabolic-limb system that is bound up with the process of will and motion, and is distinguished by processes of combustion.[68] The will process moves in the direction of death — and our human acts of will bear the character of being unfinished, pointing to the future. *Every* real act of will leads beyond itself, dying into the 'flowing ocean of the spirit'; it exceeds what is actually available as it strives towards an ideal goal, towards something greater still, and cannot reach it in the earthly realm. In fact it reaches an after-death will-sphere where it is enabled to continue working on what it began to do in the earthly realm, and is received into the cosmic Sun Realm, the only place where Goodness exists.[69]

Our human will process — the spiritual movement-forms of our life's path — point in this way irrevocably to the future. On the other hand, a central force of the past is working in the will, from the direction from which we came. Belonging unconsciously to the will there is the path into earthly incarnation, the path into a life journey, which — coming from cosmic unbornness — was way back in time, and which we worked hard to prepare.[70] Spirit-recognition 'in depths of soul' leads back to this dimension from whence the I came, which — as Rudolf Steiner says — 'lives in the will'.[71] The 'depths of soul', as the Foundation Stone meditation stresses, is where we can experience the human I's connection to our own origin, and the permanent home of our essential being (our 'coming to be') in 'God's I' — not in the transcendental 'Beyond' of conventional theology, but in the innermost part of our own soul. That is where, as Rudolf Steiner tells us, there is a 'cosmic memory' of 'what we see when we look back spiritually into the first stage of earthly man's becoming, when, as human beings, we had not yet separated off from divine/spiritual beings'.[72]

On the other hand we must keep hold of the thought that our meditative encounter with 'world creating being in depths of soul' does not apply exclusively to the past; the experience which we have to practise 'recognising' in this connection consists much more in seeing that 'the wielding will' of world creation is by no means finished, accomplished and complete, but is still an actual happening taking place constantly. What this actually means, however, is that while the I is actively 'recognising' its 'coming into being' in the I of God, it is once again 'winning back' a part of its divine, God-related being. Human beings are not 'the image of God' in a set and unequivocal way, but have to make and strengthen a connection to the sphere of their origin each time anew, i.e. to form and actively affirm it. In their 'depths of soul' they can again and again become aware of their origin, and it is essential they do so, in order truly to be in charge of their life in the will-sphere in the whole movement from the past into the future. 'And you will truly live in your body's cosmic being.'

If human beings in depths of soul again become conscious of their spiritual origin, reaching back into the sphere of cosmic unbornness, and if they acquire an awareness of the significance of their life's path, of the direction of their (unfinished) aims and tasks (which are part of everyone's being), then their being receives back again its actual connection with Spirit and World, its existence in 'the body's cosmic being'. *Every* individual 'I' can experience him or herself in this way, as willed by the gods, in their dignity, their individual character, their essential being and contribution to life as a whole — even if the various circumstances of their biography, their talents, gifts and potential are extremely different. This is an aspect of self-affirmation that individuals can experience 'in depths of soul', and in view of the dissolving of outer support will no doubt *need* to be experienced more and more.

It will at the same time become clear in this area of experience that the human faculty of will may no longer be allowed to be misused as a means of satisfying personal and private needs, or acquiring advantages and possessions; in other words, being an instrument of the civilised, technological, egocentric world destruction. Rather, it has to be recognised as the fundamental soul force that it is, the force that has guided us as individuals, into earthly existence and to our worldly tasks and worldly responsibilities, to do the kind of social 'work' that each single one of us owes to life as a whole.[73] As Rudolf Steiner tells us, in the sphere of the 'will-limb process' love is at work, the 'wielding universal love'; or, 'the being of omnipotent human and universal love'.[74] If the will becomes 'true', then human beings live their lives out of this power of love. 'I am the Way, the Truth and the Life' (John 14:6). On Maundy Thursday, before the Last Supper, Christ Jesus washed the *feet* of the disciples. 'He that is washed needeth not save to wash his feet, but is clean every whit' (John 13:10).

★

> Human soul!
> You live in the beat of heart and lung
> Which leads you through the rhythm of time
> Into the realm of your own soul's feeling:
> Practise *spirit presence*   .
> In soul composure
> Where the weaving deeds
> Of universal becoming
> Unite
> The individual I
> With the I of the World;
> And you will truly feel
> In the active life of your soul.

The second time the 'human soul' is addressed it calls to mind our own life in the middle area of the bodily organization, that is the 'beat of heart and lung'. The 'rhythmic' system, as Rudolf Steiner first described it in 1917 in his *Riddles of the Soul*, is the bearer of our soul feeling, in the way that the metabolic-limb system is the physiological basis of the unfolding of the will. The human soul lives 'in the beat of heart and lung', which, as 'the rhythm of time', leads us into and enables us to have 'our own soul feeling'. In the manner of this time rhythm, in particular the constantly modified rhythm of breathing, we are able not only to develop a feeling relationship to the being and processes of our environment, but to ourselves as well. It is through feeling that we experience the world in the centre of our being — both as the person who feels all this and also as the actual *feeler* of it. This process shapes our whole earthly biography between birth and death, and our experiences are continuously being 'conducted' into 'our own soul feeling', except during the intervals of sleep, and increasing again at death. The path into 'our own soul feeling', 'by way of the rhythm of time', ultimately means the whole course of our chronological biography and its culmination in death, leading to an intensification at death of what was taking place throughout life. The progress we go through in our development after death happens, according to Rudolf Steiner, mainly in the sphere of the feeling will.[75]

The physiological processes of the rhythmic system already have an organic connection that connects death with life in a special way. In the region of the will in the metabolic-limb-system, both breaking down processes and upbuilding (reciprocating) processes take place, whereas in the rhythmic system, in the interplay of the blood and the breathing, an intensive *fusion* takes place between life and death. The blood is enlivened afresh over and over again through the oxygen we breathe in, and over and over again, from the direction of our consciousness, the stream of death forces enters our blood and finds its way out of the organism in suffocating carbon dioxide. This is what Willem Zeylmans van Emmichoven says,[76] based on detailed descriptions by Rudolf Steiner.[77] Our 'own soul feeling' arises in the course of our life as a struggle between life and death, light and darkness, construction and destruction processes — that are mirrored on the soul level in gestures of turning towards things, or away from them, such as sympathy and antipathy, love and hate.

In this highly dynamic happening, however, the 'human soul' should, according to the Foundation Stone meditation, pause — just as it should in the lively and (mostly unconscious) life of will. Becoming aware meditatively of the will dimension in our own 'everyday' life, by doing an 'evening review' of the (past) happenings and (unfinished) intentions of the day, and, too, of the whole of our biography, opens our eyes to real life, in the joining together of what is past and what is future. On the other hand, 'spirit presence', in the realm of the human middle sphere, requires the attaining of a soul composure that rises above attraction and rejection, sympathy and antipathy, joy and sorrow, and tries to make these serve solely as organs of world perception, as Rudolf Steiner explained in detail in his spiritual-scientific study book *Knowledge of the Higher Worlds*.[78] It is, then, no longer a matter of warding off what is disagreeable or, in a hedonistic way, making pleasure and happiness our aim in life — together with the right to be able to 'get rid of lives not worth living', by way of euthanasia and assisted suicide, but to integrate in a positive way different and possibly tragic occurrences into our normal existence. In his *Phenomenology of the Spirit* Hegel wrote in Jena in 1806:

Death, if we want to use this word for such an unreality, is the most terrible thing, and to keep hold of what is dead requires the greatest strength. [...] But the life of the spirit is not the kind of life that is afraid of death, and keeps clear of being ravaged, but the kind that endures all this and thrives on it. It wins its way to becoming true by finding itself when in a state of absolutely being torn to pieces. This is not the kind of power that is positive by avoiding looking at what is negative, as though we were saying that something is nothing or wrong, and they have finished with it, leaving it to go on to something else, but it has this power only by looking at what is negative squarely in the face and staying with it. This sticking with it is the magic power that gives it existence.[79]

But this kind of turning round of existence, that goes even further than that — of turning death into life — takes place permanently in the region of the rhythmic system.

When 'soul composure' has been achieved, as the Foundation Stone meditation goes on to say, the 'weaving deeds of world becoming' unite the 'individual I', 'a person's own I', with the 'I of the World'. Through overcoming personal subjectivity, that is to say, by achieving objectivity in one's 'own' feeling, we grow beyond our inner space into the world. We become included in something larger, take a close interest in it, and actually feel part of it. At the Christmas Conference Rudolf Steiner said: 'And one can be convinced that when human beings understand the wonderful secret of the relationship between the lungs and the heart — which, when seen by inner perception, the way the world rhythms that have been active for thousands of years, beat too, in our pulse and the rhythms of our blood, ensouling us with the forces of World soul — we can hope that by grasping the wisdom of this with hearts that have become organs of knowledge we may then experience the World pictures given us by the gods, powerfully revealing to us what is there in the cosmos. Just as we grasp the prevailing World Love in our active movements we shall grasp the archetypal pictures of the World's being when we experience in ourselves the mysterious transition between the World rhythm and our human rhythm, and by means of these, the human rhythm that mysteriously takes place on a soul/spiritual level between lung and heart.'[80] The 'deeds of World becoming' are dynamic processes of creation and becoming, which are permanently taking place from out of the 'archetypal pictures of World Being'. Human beings experience their real presence in their rhythmic organization in so far as this is no longer a harbour for self-interest, but has become an actual organ for experiencing what they meet with in their environment. The mysterious rhythm processes between heart and lung, the blood and the breath, belong to the world of creating and becoming. If human beings awaken to them, they extend their own existence into the world, and connect with what is coming into being there. They experience themselves as being 'united' with it, belonging — of having a 'feeling of self-knowledge' in sharing in the spiritual course of the year, as Rudolf Steiner wrote in the preface to his *Calendar of the Soul* at Easter 1912.[81]

On the other hand our experience of being included in the 'weaving deeds of World becoming' that can take place in our centre, the experience we have of the unity of 'our own I' with the I of the World, concerns on no account only connections among the being and becoming in the natural world (such as the course of the year) but also the course of civilization in light and darkness. The 'weaving deeds of World becoming' can also turn out to be tragic events, natural disasters and catastrophes in the course of civilization, revolutions and wars, in which the destiny of individual people becomes involved, but which spiritually disciplined human beings will not wish to avoid, but be part of in heart and will. 'A huge community is spread out over the Earth. It is called suffering and strength'(Maria Krehbiel-Darmstädter). In the will sphere the 'coming into being' in 'the I of God', experienced by way of love, is a total affirmation coming from the far-distant past and can be re-affirmed time and again. When individual human beings find themselves in this 'depth of soul' they are filled with the will to work, and equipped to work in the world in a lively, creative way. The important thing is that they succeed in really *connecting* with the world, both in its becoming and in its destiny from out of their feeling soul that fully sympathises with everything taking place in other people and in the whole of the environment, i.e. experiencing the reality of a 'World I' which is beyond the boundary of 'their own I'. This is how human beings, through 'soul composure', broaden their own being and experience their environment, time, joy and hardship, and the need to participate in it all, actively.

This is how it becomes possible to make the transition from 'the body's cosmic being' to 'the active life of the soul' — the step from the initial indwelling being to independent, active participation, to working out of a real interest and connectedness of soul, a 'sharing of the destiny of the times' (Steiner).[82]

★

Human soul!
You live in the stillness of the head
Which from the founts of eternity
Disclose for you cosmic thoughts.
Practise *spirit beholding*
In thought calm
Where the eternal aims of Gods
Give the light of spirit worlds
To the individual I
For will in freedom
And you will truly *think*
In the founts of your human spirit.

Finally 'the human soul' also lives in the 'stillness of the head', the upper nerve-senses pole of the human organization, where the movement of the limbs sphere to a large extent comes to a halt. While discussing *anthropology*, Rudolf Steiner often referred to the fact that human beings lift their head organization almost entirely out of the restless movement of the limb sphere. Our life's course is eventful, and people go here, there and everywhere; our head, however, 'lords it' in comparative peace, above all the goings on. Vitality is reduced there; consciousness dominates existence. According to the Foundation Stone meditation, it is here that cosmic thoughts are disclosed from 'founts of eternity'. The meditation certainly does not say that our thoughts arise in the head or are even 'produced' there; on the contrary, the sphere where they originate transcends human beings, even transcends space and time as qualities of earthly incarnation. As Rudolf Steiner described repeatedly, it is with their limbs that human beings take part in the world of earthly space, and the limb organisation itself is composed of earthly forces.[83] In the heart and breathing organization of the rhythmic system, the 'human soul' lives in and with time; in the head, though, it takes part in the nerve-sense processes, in eternity. The head, or rather the 'human soul' that is active there, acquires access to 'eternal founts' — the acquisition of these, as Rudolf Steiner told us in detail in his works on the knowledge of science, requiring a strenuous effort of perception. Thoughts, concepts and ideas are the substance of a super personal, super earthly (cosmic) world that becomes accessible to human beings in an individual way to the extent that they actually reach out for them. If they enter actively into the thought world they acquire access to the 'World Thoughts' that are at the root of earthly existence, the ideas behind earthly 'things', their creative principle. 'When thinking grasps the idea it fuses with the archetypal ground of world existence; what is active outside then enters into the human spirit. We become one with the objective reality at its highest potency. *Real human communion is the becoming aware of the actual nature of ideas in their reality.* The relation thinking has to ideas is the same as eyes have to light and the ears to sound. It is the organ that apprehends it'.[84] As Steiner already expounded in his earlier publications on the theory of knowledge, human beings add the conceptual aspect to the world of sense perception by means of their thinking. By doing this they connect something that inherently belongs together, and is divided solely within their own organization just because this organization is there: namely percept and idea (concept). In that 'human souls', with the help of their head organization in which they live, disclose World thoughts, they can, under earthly circumstances, truly think, i.e. add to the sensual aspect of things the spiritual part belonging to them.

By means of the more-than-spatial and more-than-temporal quality of what the head organization attains to — ideas — human beings belong through the earthly realm to the cosmos. Their limbs lead them through the world of space, enabling them to have a meaningful biography, perform all their karmic deeds and go through their karmic sufferings, experience old and new destiny — which, after death, becomes part of the cosmos. With the accomplishments of their middle organization, human beings expand into their environment, into the periphery; they become social beings with a feeling interest in what they encounter which, after their earthly biography is finished, lead their earthly experience on into eternity. Their limbs connect human beings 'downwards' with the Earth, the chest and breathing organization with the environment, whereas the spherical head — that mirrors the cosmos — is organized 'upwards', and by its means heaven comes on to the Earth in the re-connecting of creation with its spirituality, the sense world with the Logos. From below upwards, from our feet to our head, human beings awaken to the incarnating of the Foundation Stone meditation.[85]

The 'disclosing' of 'World thoughts', which is the finding of real concepts or ideas of things, is already a demanding process that has to be done with will. The Foundation Stone meditation says it has to be practised, but in the realm of thinking it can and should mean much more:

Practise spirit beholding
In thought calm
Where the eternal aims of Gods
Give the light of spirit worlds
To the individual I
For will in freedom;

In 'thought calm' our thinking can carry out the step to Imagination, to the 'seeing' spirit. This is the way in which, in spiritual perception — under the influence of thought calm — the force can enter that, in the form of 'the light of spirit worlds', leads the earthly occurrences into the future, corresponding to an intention of the world process of creation and creative powers. In his basic scientific works, which culminated in his *Philosophy of Freedom* (1894), Rudolf Steiner described human understanding not only as a 'steady penetration into the grounds of worlds'[86] but emphasised that, in the encounter with 'the spirit depths', human beings can receive Intuitions — a situation that is called for at a given moment, as fair treatment, in an actual life situation or problem. The human will as such is by no means free, but if human beings by means of moral Imagination — 'beholding the spirit' — acquire Intuitions of right actions and make them conscious motives of their intentions, they are dealing with it in freedom. They are promoting the world process, World Becoming in the sense of 'the eternal aims of Gods', and at the same time in the sense of true humanity, which is a central interest of the divine/spiritual world. The practice of 'spirit beholding' in 'thought calm' is the prerequisite for contributing to world progress in a proper, constructive and healthy way, and lies within the intentions of creation.

The light that is approached in this way is the 'light of the world', 'the light of spirit worlds', and as such is the only thing able to shine from out of the darkness into the true future. Human beings on the path of development receive this spirit light from the world order as a 'gift' to their ego, to use in freedom. Here in this area the individuality is not tied from the start ('the individual I comes to being in the I of God') or, through sympathetic interest, united with the 'I of the world'; on the contrary, it actually acts freely, out of nothingness, at the start of something new that it is just creating. Human beings are able to be productive and creative as independent, creative beings in whom the spiritual world both trusts and confides. They can genuinely bring moral Intuitions and impulses into the earthly world, planting them here to stay, and making a real impact on life. The Intuitions we have mentally grasped can become our leading ideals, reaching into our limb/will sphere, and bringing them into the world through our actions. Through connecting with the middle sphere our heart processes become involved; here the ideas connect up with the realm of the feelings, and moving into the will processes they attain to the stage of ideals.[87] Rudolf Steiner said at the Christmas Conference: 'When human beings will be able to bring the right manner of feeling perception to what is being revealed in their head system, in a state of rest on their shoulders, even whilst they are walking, then, feeling themselves in their head system, pouring their heart's warmth into their head system, they will be able to experience the living activity of cosmic thoughts in their own being.'[88] This is how human beings eventually reach with their ego to the attainment of free will which they experience meditatively — starting with 'true' thinking that is connected with 'founts of eternity', that discloses cosmic thoughts and is able to set them in the right direction. 'And you will truly think in the fount of your human spirit.'

★

The triple practice, in the direction of 'truly' living (in the will) the feeling and the thinking, leads to recalling and increasing the forces of the soul, to purifying and strengthening them. They at the same time open up, in soul deepening, the way to the spiritual background and to the real relationship in which 'true' thinking, feeling and will stand in the whole course of our lives, its chronology, its space dimension and eternal direction. Into all this flows the active participation of the ego, out of the past, in the present and in the developing of a future that allows for an increasing responsibility for oneself and for one's freedom. If human beings stride, with full recall and active participation, through the various realms of experience connected with these, the cosmos will, in a certain respect, give answer: 'Anthroposophy is a path of knowledge that wants to lead the spirit of man to the spirit in the universe', Rudolf Steiner wrote in his first anthroposophical guideline after the Christmas Conference.[89] This 'leading' of the soul and spirit to the cosmic spirit prepares the way for the soul exercises, both in regard to the experience of the 'individual I' *in* the 'I of God', which opens up in the soul's depths, as well as the uniting of the I with the 'I of the World'. With this comes the experiencing of the 'gift' of the aims of the Gods in thinking, leading from the inner space of the soul and spirit into far spheres — and finally to the self-knowledge of the human I in the divine Trinity. Yet in the corresponding passages of the three verses there is not yet any mention of the cosmos, but only of what is experienced as World principle *in* our own soul and spirit. Rudolf Steiner spoke of 'pronouncements about World secrets in so far as these World secrets resurrect in human souls as human self-knowledge'.

However, the step from microcosm to macrocosm does follow in the course of the meditation — the triple call to the human soul is followed by the description of the event that 'corresponds' cosmically to each process in human beings. Following on from the description of the will-limb sphere to the 'coming to being' of the I in the 'I of God' and to existence in 'the body's cosmic being', we are told:

> For the Father Spirit of the heights is present
> In world depths begetting existence
> Seraphim, Cherubim, Thrones,
> May there ring forth from the heights
> The call re-echoed in the depths
> Proclaiming: Humankind is born of God.
> The elemental spirits hear it
> In east, west, north, south,
> *May hu*man beings *hear* it!

The 'human soul' can, and must, achieve 'spirit recognition', so as to penetrate through to the true realm of its will, meaning its whole existence, into those depths of the soul 'where in the wielding will of World creating the individual I comes to being in the I of God'. This is, however, only possible for the soul to do because this soul process corresponds to a cosmic process in the general human dimension, which is disclosed as the meditation proceeds. This is where the 'wielding will of World creation' in soul depths exists and is to be found, *because* the 'Father Spirit of the heights', the creative Father Principle of the divine Trinity, moves through the world 'begetting existence'. Humankind as a whole (including the archetypal body of human beings)[90] belongs within the Foundation Stone meditation and also within the world, to begotten existence. Rudolf Steiner translates the Rosicrucian statement 'Ex deo nascimur' in the Foundation Stone meditation in connection with 'humankind is born of God'. The individual ego comes to being in the 'I of God', and the 'Father Spirit of the heights' constantly moves through the depths of Earth existence (and the human soul).

'Humankind is born of God', 'Ex deo nascimur' are, Rudolf Steiner says, the way the 'cosmic word' speaks. There rings forth from it the fire of love, the wisdom, the power of sacrifice of the first hierarchy to be involved in a special way in creating the world. The constant birth of humankind from the 'Father God' is accomplished with the help of these qualities of the Seraphim, Cherubim and Thrones, and it is a part of each of the macrocosmic verses that the hierarchies are directly addressed in a prayerful request: 'May ...'. The intervention of the hierarchies in the cosmic Word, which includes the spiritually-supported process of the educating of human beings and of humankind, should also be maintained in periods of earthly alienation and destruction in which the life and the continuation of humanity have been more doubtful than ever before. The prayerful request is that the cosmic Word and the hierarchies at work in it remain, both now and in the future — despite the hubris of modern gene technology and the genetic manipulation of people ('who should play God if not us?')[91] — clearly audible on Earth, and that the spiritually-supported process of creation can continue to find its earthly answer in the future, in the form of human beings who are responsible both in themselves and in their actions.

The cosmic Word and the creative origin of humankind in the Father God are 'heard' all over the earthly world (in east, west, north and south) by the elemental spirits. The Foundation Stone meditation is speaking, however, of the outlook and hope that ever more human beings will develop a conscious hearing of the cosmic Word and the wielding of spirit in the physically/earthly realm, so that it will still continue to be permanently active against the powerful claims of materialism. Wielding is a word, which, according to Zeylmans, expresses in its sounds a force that creates from out of the spirit, actually bearing within it an active, creative force.[92]

Human beings individually can, in the first verse of the Foundation Stone meditation, awaken in their own will — awaken to all that works in them from the past to the future, connecting them at the level of being in their very substance, with the principle of the Father God of creation, and setting their whole being in the right relationship to the world around them, in their 'body's cosmic being'. Individuals can practise this on their own, because the same applies to the whole of humankind ('in the consciousness of our own humanity we feel our way into the divine Father'). To portray this connection as a whole, and at the same time to ask the spiritual/cosmic powers to continue to help and encourage humanity, covers the whole content of the macrocosmic lines to do with the will.

★

After the call to achieve 'true feeling' in 'soul composure', and the uniting of our own individual I with the 'I of the World' and the destiny of the environment, both in life and death, and the binding participation in 'the active life of your soul', the following cosmic verse follows:

> For the Christ Will is present all around
> In world rhythms shedding grace on our souls;
> Kyriotetes, Dynamis, Exusiai,
> May what is formed by the west
> Have been quickened in the light of the east,
> Proclaiming:
> In Christo morimur.
> The elemental spirits hear it
> In east, west, north and south:
> *May hu*man beings *hear* it!

Since the Mystery of Golgotha, the passage through earthly death and the resurrection after 'three days', Christ has been actively at work in the earthly environment or 'periphery'; here, within the breathing of the Earth, he is wielding power, restoring, enlivening and healing, assisting the Earth to 'become a sun', supporting and bringing order into people's destinies — in their earthly biographies and in the after-death existence, 'in world rhythms shedding grace on our souls'. *'The power of Christ* that works everywhere in the periphery, that is alive in the air encircling the Earth . . . .' (Steiner).[93]

With the coming of Christ from the Sun sphere down to the Earth, which culminated in the event of Golgotha and gave a new quality to earthly events, our human relationship to time changed. From the sphere of the Sun, the source of cosmic rhythms, the Christ brought us a new experience of chronology (including that of biography) into earthly existence.[94] Not until these events took place, at 'the turning of the times', did the temporal aspects of human life on Earth acquire that specific form and significance which has characterised it since then. Right up to today, the time element governing the rhythmic organization, the blood and breathing organism has been closely related to the Christ Mystery, as Rudolf Steiner often spoke of.[95] In an essay which Rudolf

Steiner wrote later for Ita Wegman and the circle of 'young medics' associated with her, when he was on his sickbed, Rudolf Steiner went once again through the aspects connected with this, and described the breath stream as a more delicate repetition of man's descent from the spiritual realms into the physical world at birth, and the bloodstream moving towards the heart as the 'aspiration of individual existence towards cosmic existence'; and he went on to say:

> The blood of the heart aspiring towards the breath in the lungs, is man's aspiring towards the cosmos. The air we breathe aspiring towards the heart's blood is man being blessed by the cosmos. Blood striving towards the heart is a refined dying process. Blood as carbon dioxide striving to be breathed out represents a refined death process. In the human blood stream there constantly streams up to the cosmos a process that is radically shaped according to a death pattern, as the force in the blood takes hold of the whole of the physical organism. [...] The Christ Mystery is the revealing of the great miracle that takes place *between* the heart and the lungs: The cosmos becomes man; man becomes the cosmos. [...] That which streams from the lungs to the heart is the human correlation of the descent of Christ to the Earth; that which works forcefully from the heart to the lungs is the human correlation of the passing of human beings after death, through the Christ Impulse, into the spiritual world. In this respect the Mystery of Golgotha lives in the organic pattern between the heart and the lungs.[96]

★

In so far as human beings awaken in the physiological centre of their rhythmic organism, in the interpenetration of life and death, to a feeling of their own being, and at the same time participate in their human environment, then looked at from an earthly/cosmic point of view they are active within the realm of Christ's activities since Golgotha. '*In Christ death becomes life*' is how Rudolf Steiner translated the Latin words 'In Christo morimur'. According to him, between the heart and the lungs we can experience — in the processes and rhythms at work there — not only 'world rhythms' that have been active for thousands of years, for aeons, continuing on in the pulse and rhythm of the blood, and awakening in us a feeling of belonging to World existence, but — as well as that — a feeling for being human and belonging to humanity as a whole can take hold of us in an intimately Christian way. In a feeling way, deeply touching and transforming their own rhythms, human beings come in touch with the destiny of the Age, both as individuals and as members of the whole race. Zeylmans wrote:

> [The Christ] Will is present in the world rhythms, and all human hearts have been taken up into these in the selfsame rhythms. You may have a go at meditating on a picture of a huge wave of rhythms passing over the whole surface of the Earth, containing all the individual human rhythms of heart and lungs. Rudolf Steiner often referred to the connection existing between our human heartbeat and the cosmic rhythms of day, our age of life, and the Platonic Year. Although all the various blood rhythms show slight variations, they all of them come from one universal rhythm. If we bear in mind that our heart is the only organ that is really on Earth, we can certainly see this wave, that is moving round the Earth and that beats in all our hearts together, as having to do with creating the making of a new Earth. All round us the Earth is dying to arise anew in human souls, and a beginning of newly arisen Earth is to be found in the sounding together of the rhythms that are building the basis for a new humanity. Christ's Will is active in the Earth's periphery: that is, in the totality of human beings who populate our Earth.[97]

The rhythmic system and the Christ Will associated with it in the 'periphery' are active in the direction of a humanity-building unity; they belong together in carrying and bearing our common destiny. In 'the active life of the soul' this interconnection (of the 'individual I', you/we and the 'I of the World') is active and can lead to a new impulse of creating and forming on Earth — to a continuation to what has become history in the direction of the active 'Christ Impulse' (Steiner). These creative, upbuilding processes of the social future pass through processes of death and of resurrection and need fire forces, forces of sacrifice and form forces in the sense of the Second Hierarchy, the one connected with the Christ, and their assistance is being asked for. The Christ being, who is present in the world as Spirit Word, and who took the path of humanity from the Orient to the Occident,[98] leads, according to Zeylmans, the fire forces from the east to the form forces of the west, and that '. . . through the fact that he [the Christ] is moving in this stream from east to west, the death forces, working as form forces from the west, are overcome by higher forces of life.'[99] All these interlinking circumstances live in the achieving of 'the active life of our soul' from out of the forces of 'true feeling' — the kind of feeling that unites with the Christ and suffers destruction for the sake of what is developing in a positive direction. In their rhythmic organization human beings are permanently going through life and death; from out of the Mystery of Christ's Resurrection they are active in the central part of their being as individuals, but even more as members of a social community that is a preliminary step towards the humanitarian world community of the future. 'In Christ death becomes life': The elemental spirits over the whole Earth 'hear' the 'Christ Sun'[100] and human beings can acquire the goodwill to awaken in this sense to the Cosmic Word.

★

The third microcosmic verse of the Foundation Stone meditation concerns human (head) thinking and its true quality as world thinking that succeeds in disclosing and understanding the intentions of divine/spiritual beings (i.e. the intentions of the creation) and that base it on individual action in freedom. The 'active life of the soul', in and coming from the sphere of the rhythmic organization, the formative, creative forces from the human centre, require guiding intentions to be able to realise in a universally just way what is right and fitting for our times. The 'true' *life* of action (readiness to act) and 'true' *feeling* (awareness of the destiny of the times) need the right ideas, 'true' *thinking*, in order to make an impact in the world that is positive.

With regard to the cosmic aspect of the meditative path to acquiring 'true thinking', and the freewill this makes possible, the Foundation Stone meditation tells us:

> For the Spirit's cosmic thoughts are present
> In world existence begging for light
> Archai, archangeloi, angeloi,
> May there ascend from the depths
> The plea heard in the heights;
> Proclaiming:
> In the spirit's cosmic thoughts the soul will awaken.
> The elemental spirits hear it
> In east, west, north, south;
> *May hu*man beings *hear* it!

The 'Father spirit of the heights' holds sway in 'world depths' begetting existence; the Christ Will holds sway in the periphery of the Earth, in world rhythms shedding grace on our souls; regarding 'the spirit's cosmic thoughts', referring to the third principle of the divine trinity, the Holy Spirit whose arrival Christ announced to his disciples in his farewell words and who began being active at the Whitsun Festival, the Foundation Stone meditation tells us that here too the Holy Spirit holds sway: the spirit's cosmic thoughts hold sway in world existence, 'begging for light'. The light, which the cosmic thoughts need to be able to be active in future creation, is the light of the 'enlightened heads' — of human beings who spiritualise their thinking, i.e. make it 'real' in the sense of it becoming an active organ of perception of cosmic light. Light-filled human thinking, that is connected to the light-filled heart, is alone in a position to understand the 'spirit's cosmic thoughts', the real 'spirit light', and therefore able to understand and embrace 'the eternal aims of gods'. In other places Rudolf Steiner extensively described cosmic thoughts of the spirit as the 'cosmic intelligence' administered by Michael. Rudolf Steiner described in an imaginative picture Michael moving through the flow of time, his very being shining forth in the cosmic light.[101] He prepares human hearts and heads for the light, the 'shining power of thought', by bringing Sun forces into human evolution.

For the succeeding of this process, not only Michael, but the whole third hierarchy to which he belongs, are appealed to for help — the hierarchy of the 'Spirits of Soul', the archai, archangeloi, and the angeloi who have a special connection to human thinking. The appeal intensifies, consisting of begging to be given, 'from the depths', what will be 'heard in the heights'. Rudolf Steiner repeatedly said that the right attitude of a spiritual scientist, despite all the inner activity involved, would have to be and remain an expectant, inviting one. (Every word of anthroposophy is, fundamentally, if it is said in the right manner, a plea, a reverent invitation: begging the spirit to turn in our direction and descend to us).[102] The positive thoughts within our reach cannot, despite the urgency with which civilization needs them in the general misery of the times, be forced; on the contrary, what is required here on Earth is that we first carry out intensive preparation, which means that we go through a time of selfless 'participation in the destiny of our times', which then motivates us to approach our questions and our riddles with the greatest humility, begging and inviting a response. 'Blessed are the poor in spirit, for theirs is the kingdom of heaven' (Mt 5:5).[103]

This is the way in which the third hierarchy of spirits of soul can be of decisive help to us. If we succeed step by step, then individuals, but also the community, will come alive in the realm of the activity of 'per spiritum sanctum reviviscimus': 'In the Spirit's cosmic thoughts the soul will awaken.' By means of this soul awakening, a new thinking that is world shaping — piercing through the depths — the future of man and of humanity, will become possible.

★

Concerning the idea of the threefold human being that is at the very centre of the Foundation Stone meditation, Willem Zeylmans van Emmichoven wrote:

> It is the concept of God from which the bodily/soul/spiritual organization of the human being has arisen and will arise again anew. In the Foundation Stone meditation this concept comes to the highest form of expression. It is the first time in the history of humankind that an idea exactly expresses anatomically, physiologically as well as psychologically the being of Man, and offers at the same time the greatest meditative content.[104]

Assuming that the human body and its especial values is the 'goal set by God' (Oetinger), the Foundation Stone meditation unfolds the idea of threefold man comprehensively: it arises in the meditant, who is taken into account as the person concerned, appealing to a higher level of self-knowledge and giving encouragement. It arises also the other way round: in everybody the meditant associates with, in the respective 'other' in whom the face of a human being, as meant in the Foundation Stone meditation, is recognised — and if need be has to be helped to his feet again. It arises in this way also in the community, and can become its centre. (To find oneself in the spirit means uniting people.)[105]

The Foundation Stone meditation leads to self-awareness in a world where one loses oneself, in which spiritual/social relationships and concerns become rapidly lost, and an incomparable disturbance in identity comes about. With regard to the modern person whom the Foundation Stone meditation is addressing, Hermann Poppelbaum spoke of this as an appeal to 'someone who is walking in their sleep'. 'This is how anthroposophy appeals to people, to make them aware of themselves and to notice what they have lost.'[106] The appeal is to remind us of what we have lost, and what we can acquire afresh; it draws our attention to connections that we can discover again, and can be experienced consciously — in body, soul and spirit, in ourselves and in the cosmos. The threefold human being of the Foundation Stone meditation is, as such, the ideal human being intended by the gods, by the divine/spiritual worlds,[107] and at the same time it is the actual reality of each single human being. 'Yes, this is what I am as a human being of the spiritual world.' According to Rudolf Steiner, this experience ought to be joined to the experience of the Foundation Stone meditation — it finally leads to the understanding, the affirmation and love of the being of man, to 'anthroposophy' in the midst of all that is modern, that has been and is affecting us largely in a dehumanising way, '. . . so that human qualities do not apply any more to us human beings' (Hölderlin).[108] Speaking about the general aims of anthroposophical spiritual science Rudolf Steiner once said:

> What is enkindled in us by anthroposophical spiritual science aimed towards the supersensible realm is human love that teaches us about our human worth and helps us feel our human dignity.
>
> The knowledge of human worth, our feeling of human dignity, the will to act out of human love, these are the most beautiful of life's fruits that develop in human beings through experiencing the results of spiritual science.[109]

The 'knowledge of human value'; the 'feeling of human dignity' and 'the will to act out of human love' would have been urgently needed in the humanly disastrous depths of the twentieth century, the decades of the concentration camps and the torture, racial selection, euthanasia and mass murder — and the Foundation Stone meditation sought to contribute as a practical help to save the form of man out of the threatening depths, to help us arise anew from within. 'Is that a human being?', asked Primo Levi in the form of a paradigm, after surviving the Auschwitz concentration camp. 'Ecce homo — Behold the man!', Pilate had stressed, almost 2000 years earlier, regarding the tortured Christ (John: 19.5).

★

In response to the many questions and challenges bound up with the twentieth century Rudolf Steiner gave his answer in the form of the Foundation Stone meditation formulated in 1923, and with the Dornach School of Spiritual Science, even though culture as a whole largely ignored these contributions. That this was the case is by no means surprising, for what Rudolf Steiner was preparing was different from what prevailed in the twentieth century (and prevails still). Steiner himself spoke of the coming of a new epoch and a future culture of 'self-lessness',[110] and the Foundation Stone meditation belongs essentially to this. The overcoming of this materialistic selfishness, the eradicating from the whole of civilization of this 'putting of the blame on other people' (Steiner)[111] which, if it continues, would bring about the destruction of planet Earth — and the bringing about instead of a 'recognised self-lessness' (Steiner) are part of a process of development of which the Foundation Stone meditation is a good example.

If this path is followed, then the figure of the Christ will come to meet each individual person in a new way, above the level of confessions. For Rudolf Steiner, and within the whole of anthroposophical spiritual science, Christ is the Representative or the I of Humanity. Christ speaks to the truly human part of a person, he confirms their humanity, and does so in an absolutely unconditional way. He is the 'Lord of the heavenly forces on Earth' who, at the turning of the times, took on human form so as to be able to share and accompany humankind's future paths of destiny — through life, death and resurrection. Christ and 'christianised human beings' form the central part of the Foundation Stone meditation. With the Christ as the 'Representative and the I of humanity' culture has a future, even if the conscious experience of the Christ has been granted at present to comparatively few people — in contrast to the nature beings who know more and different things. Concerning Rudolf Steiner's statement in connection with the Foundation Stone meditation (or one of its 'rhythms') the elemental spirits of east, west, north and south would be able to 'hear' the Christ Sun. Willem Zeylmans van Emmichoven wrote:

> The Mystery of Golgotha has connected the Christ with the Earth; he lives in the world of the etheric forces in which the elemental spirits are present as living beings. They have already taken the events of Golgotha into themselves. May human beings hear it! That is the task [...] to live our way into nature where the Christ now dwells, and to learn there, together with the elemental beings, to understand the Christ light as the creative Word of an Earth that is becoming new.[112]

Regarding the closing fourth verse of the Foundation Stone meditation, Zeylmans wrote:

> In the closing words all this becomes a deeply heartfelt prayer of the human soul, that in future this divine Light, this Christ Sun, may help humanity to develop.[113]

The development of human beings *and* of humankind, with the help of the Christ Light, the Christ Sun, to become the central point of a true selfless humanity, was and is indeed the main concern of the whole of the Foundation Stone meditation. The evolution of individual human beings in the direction of true thinking, feeling and will is a Christ-centred evolution, which in the words of Sergei O. Prokofieff is being introduced and initiated by the Christ.[114] It leads from the distortions of the twentieth century over to restoring what human beings are actually meant to be in respect to body, soul and spirit. Rudolf Steiner described in lectures how problematic the situation was at the turning of the times, 2,000 years ago, with regard to the physical body and ego consciousness, which was followed by the Christ incarnation in the Mystery of Golgotha, and the forming of the 'incorruptible' resurrection body. It brought about a complete re-arising of the lost principles of human evolution (Steiner).[115] The Foundation Stone meditation refers to this event and what became possible at Golgotha; its effectiveness, however, does not require a new incarnation of a God, but takes place from out of the human I, which (by means of the meditation) seeks an inner connection to Christ and to the spirit body that he has recovered, cosmically established, and proceeds with it into the future.[116]

As the actual achieving of our full humanity, this step in evolution is at the same time the prerequisite for a new union of individual people on a higher level, in the sense of an esoteric community that carries the destiny of humanity as a whole — in each individual ego. 'The ego of man is being made ready to be the bearer of the ego of humankind. The individual becomes the human race; humanity lives as a whole in each individual'. 'In so far as individual human beings bear Christ within them, in so far as the ego of humankind lives in them, they are to that extent the whole of humanity' (Willem Zeylmans van Emmichoven).[117] In 1956, decades before the first nuclear disasters and major ecological catastrophes of the second half of the twentieth century, Zeylmans wrote in the spirit of the Foundation Stone meditation:

> Things have progressed to the point today that in an external sense humanity has already become one; no significant events occur that, in so far as they happen on Earth, do not in a direct or an indirect way concern everyone. Therefore it is now our task to become a united humanity in a deeper sense.[118]

'In the Spirit's cosmic thoughts the soul will awaken.' 'One can also say: The soul awakens in the spirit of humanity.'[119] It is surely with such an

understanding of 'humanity', that is, on the basis of having successively
achieved becoming human, that we will, in future, be capable of both
living life on Earth and surviving beyond it; and it will be due to the
selflessness arising from it that will enable us to form out of the forces of
love a new 'body' in which the etheric Christ can live.[120]

★

At the end of the Foundation Stone meditation Rudolf Steiner turned his
attention back to the original Christmas night at the turning of the times
and created a closing fourth verse, which — as he said — gathers it
altogether in our hearts;[121] 'bringing it altogether in the remembering of
the event of Golgotha that gives to the whole of evolution its meaning'.[122] Rudolf Steiner gave the Foundation Stone meditation to his
pupils on Christmas Day, 25 December 1923. The mantram was to be
enlivening and *inspiring* for the coming time and its tasks,[123] for people who
were ready to give their whole work and destiny to the twentieth century
and develop their spiritual initiative as 'helpers of the stream of world
evolution' carried by the Christ Will.[124] For this they needed, and will
need, true thinking, feeling and will, the Christ Warmth and the Christ
Light, freedom and love, to be able both individually and as a community
to bring up-building forces into a disastrous world.

At the turning of time
Cosmic Spirit Light descended
Into the earthly stream of being;
Darkness of night
Had run its course;
The light of day
Shone forth in human souls:
Light
That gives warmth
To poor shepherds' hearts,
Light
That enlightens
The wise heads of kings.
God-given light,
Christ Sun
Give warmth
To our hearts;
Give light
To our heads;
That what we found
From our hearts
What we guide
From our heads
Will be good.

1

Menschenseele!
Du lebest in den Gliedern
Die dich durch die Raumeswelt
Im Geistermeereswesen tragen:
Übe Geist-Erinnern
In Seelentiefen
Wo in waltendem
Weltenschöpfer-Sein
Das eigne Ich
Im Gottes-Ich
Erweset
Und du wirst wahrhaft leben
Im Menschen-Welten-Wesen.

Menschenseele!
Du lebest in dem Herzens-Lungen-Schlage
Der dich durch den Zeitenrhythmus
Ins eigne Seelenwesensfühlen leitet:
Übe Geist-Besinnen
Im Seelengleichgewichte
Wo die wogenden
Welten-Werde-Taten

The verses of the mantram in the original German, in Rudolf Steiner's own handwriting

2

Das eigne Ich
Dem ~~Gottes~~ Welten - Ich
Vereinen
Und du wirst wahrhaft fühlen
Im Menschen - Seelen - Wirken.

Menschenseele!
Du lebst im ruhenden Haupte
Das dir aus Ewigkeitsgründen
Die Weltgedanken erschliesset:
Übe Geist - Erschauen
In Gedanken - Ruhe

Wo die ew'gen Götterziele
Welten - Wesens - Licht
Dem eignen Ich
Zu freiem Wollen
Schenken
Und du wirst wahrhaft denken
Im Menschen - Geistes - Gründen.

3.

In der Zeitenwende
Trat das Welten-Geistes-Licht
In den irdischen Wesensstrom;
Nacht-Dunkel hatte ausgewaltet
Taghelles Licht
Erstrahlte in Menschenseelen

Licht, das erwärmet
Die armen Hirten ~~herzen~~
Licht, das erleuchtet
Die weisen Königshäupter –

Göttliches Licht
Christus-Sonne
erwärme unsre Herzen
Erleuchte unsre Häupter

Dass gut werde
Was wir aus Herzen
gründen
aus Häuptern
zielvoll führen wollen.

4.

Denn es waltet der Vater-Geist der Höhen
In den Weltentiefen Sein-erzeugend

S. ch. Th.

Lasset aus den Höhen erklingen
Was in den Tiefen das Echo findet:

Das spricht:

E. D. n.

Das hören die
Elementengeister
im
O. W. N. S.

Menschen mögen es
hören.

Denn es waltet der Christus-Wille im Umkreis
In den Weltenrhythmen Seelen-begnadend

x. x.
K. J. E.

Lasset vom Osten befeuern
Was durch den Westen sich gestaltet:

Das spricht.

J. ch. M.

5.

Denn es walten des Geistes - Weltgedanken

Im Weltenwesen Licht - erflehend

A. AA. A.

Esset aus den Tiefen erbitten

Was in den Höhen erhöret wird :'

Das spricht.

P. S. S. R.

Notes

'GA' = *Gesamtausgabe* or Collected Works. For a list of English translations see page 77.

1. Rudolf Steiner, GA 260a, Dornach 1987, p. 115. Reference to Rudolf Steiner, GA 240, Dornach 1992, p. 183.
2. Friedrich Schiller: *Ausgang aus dem Leben*, edited by Peter-André Alt, Albert Meier and Wolfgang Riedel, Volume 1, Munich 2004, p. 243.
3. Georg Wilhelm Friedrich Hegel: *Phänomenologie des Geistes*, Volume 3, Frankfurt am Main, 1986, p. 35.
4. See Peter Selg: *Rudolf Steiner's Intentions for the Anthroposophical Society*, Great Barrington, 2011.
5. Rudolf Steiner: GA 182, Dornach 1996, p. 84.
6. See Rudolf Steiner: GA 259, and Peter Selg: 'Das Schicksalsjahr 1923. Rudolf Steiners Weg zur Weihnachtstagung in 1923', in Sergei O. Prokofieff and Peter Selg, *Die Weihnachstagung und die Begründung der Neuen Mysterien*, Arlesheim 2011, p.11–38. (English: see *The Creative Power of Anthroposophical Christology*.)
7. Rudolf Steiner: GA 260a, p. 115.
8. Sergei O. Prokofieff: *Die Grundsteinmeditation, Ein Schlüssel zu den neuen christlichen Mysterien*, Dornach 2003, p. 11 (English: *The Foundation Stone Meditation*, Temple Lodge 2006). Regarding the fundamental difference between the Foundation Stone meditation and the nature of the Foundation Stone, see in particular Sergei O. Prokofieff: *Menschen mögen es hören, Das Mysterium der Weihnachtstagung*, Stuttgart 2002, p. 116ff. (English: *May Human Beings Hear It!*), Temple Lodge 2004.
9. Willem Zeylmans van Emmichoven: *The Foundation Stone*, Temple Lodge 2002, and Sergei O. Prokofieff: *Rudolf Steiner and the Founding of the New Mysteries*, Temple Lodge 1994; *May Human Beings Hear It!*, Temple Lodge 2004, *The Foundation Stone Meditation*, Temple Lodge 2006.
10. Sergei O. Prokofieff: *Rudolf Steiner and the Founding of the New Mysteries*, Temple Lodge 1994, see Introduction 'How I Came to Write the Book...'.
11. Willem Zeylmans van Emmichoven: 'Rudolf Steiner in Holland', in: M. J. Krûck von Poturzyn (editor), *Wir erlebten Rudolf Steiner*, Stuttgart 1967, p. 265.
12. Paul Celan: *Gesammelte Werke in fünf Banden*, Beda Allemann and Stefan Reichert (editors), Volume 3, Frankfurt am Main, 1983, p. 185.
13. Willem Zeylmans van Emmichoven: *Der Grundstein*, Stuttgart 1990, p. 10 (English: *The Foundation Stone*, Temple Lodge 2002).

14. 'One can really not continue to live in a way befitting human dignity since the twentieth century without waking up to the reality of spiritual existence, so as to be able, from then on, to form one's life anew. What does this mean? It is saying that, from the twentieth century onwards, initiation as a principle, as one's task, can no longer remain beyond the requirements of civilization, as the source of inspiration for the few, but must become part of civilization and help to change it. Anthroposophy is not just a personal matter ... but is out of global historic necessity a task awaiting humankind.' Jörgen Smit: *Geistesschulung und Lebenspraxis*, Dornach 1969, p. 30.

15. See, among others, Athys Floride: *Stufen der Meditation, Die Grundstein-Meditation als Lebensquell*, Dornach 1987; Rudolf Grosse: *Die Weihnacht-stagung als Zeitenwende*, Dornach 1981; Jörgen Smit: *Geistesschulung und Lebenspraxis, Die Grundstein-Meditation als Zukunftsimpuls*, Dornach 1987, as well as the collected contributions of various authors in: Sergei O. Prokofieff (editor) *Die Grundsteinmeditation als Schulungsweg, Das Wirken der Weihnachtstagung in 80 Jahren*, Dornach 2002.

16. Rudolf Steiner, as quoted by Sergei.O. Prokofieff in *Menschen mögen es hören*, p. 216 (English: *May Human Beings Hear It!*, Temple Lodge 2004).

17. Rudolf Grosse: *Die Weihnachtstagung als Zeitenwende*, Dornach 1981, p. 150 (English: *The Christmas Foundation; Beginning of a New Cosmic Age*, Steiner Book Centre, 1984).

18. Sergei O. Prokofieff: *Rudolf Steiner und die Grundlegung der Neuen Mysterien*, p. 327 (English: *Rudolf Steiner and the Founding of the New Mysteries*).

19. See among others Peter Selg: 'Die geistige Dimension des Menschen? Zur Entwicklung der medizinischen Anthropologie im 20. Jahrhundert', in: Peter Heusser and Peter Selg: *Das Leib-Seele-Problem, Zur Entwicklung eines geistgemäßen Menschenbildes in der Medizin des 20. Jahrhunderts*, Arlesheim 2011, p. 80ff.

20. To help with an approach to the Foundation Stone meditation, Rudolf Steiner gave at the time of the Christmas Conference a few (short) 'rhythms' from the four verses, which can be meditated on. Regarding the significance of these 'rhythms' see among other things Willem Zeylmans van Emmichoven's studies on 'The seven Rhythms', in *Der Grundstein*, Stuttgart 1990, p. 55–64 (English: *The Foundation Stone*); Sergei O. Prokofieff: 'Die Rhythmen der Weihnachtstagung' in *Menschen mögen es hören. Das Mysterium der Weihnachtstagung*, p. 205–311 (English: *May Human Beings Hear It!*); Hans Peter van Manen: 'Die Tage der Woche und die sieben Rhythmen des Grundsteinspruches' in Sergei O. Prokofieff (editor): *Die Grundsteinmeditation als Schulungsweg, Das Wirken der Weihnachtstagung in 80 Jahren*, Dornach 2002, p. 253–281; Emanuel Zeylmans van Emmichoven: 'Die sieben Rhythmen' in: *Die Erkraftung des Herzens, Eine Mys-*

terienschulung der Gegenwart, Rudolf Steiners Zusammenarbeit mit Ita Wegman, Cordula Zeylmans van Emmichoven, Arlesheim 2009, p. 205–223.

21. See GA 264, 1996, p. 324.
22. Quoted from Peter Selg, *Maria Krehbiel-Darmstädter, Von Gurs nach Auschwitz. Der innere Weg,* Arlesheim 2010, p. 327f. All the further quotations from Maria Krehbiel-Darmstädter are taken from this biographical study.
23. Martha Besag, op. cit., p.136.
24. Hilda Besag, op. cit., pg.12.
25. Viktor E.Frankl: . . . *trotzdem Ja zum Leben sagen. Ein Psychologe erlebt das Konzentrationslager,* München 1997, p. 139. Compare this with Peter Selg: *Überleben in Auschwitz. Elie Wiesel, Ruth Klüger, Ruth Elias, Primo Levi, Viktor Frankl,* Arlesheim 2010.
26. Quoted from Christian Feldmann: *Elie Wiesel — ein Leben gegen die Gleichgültigkeit,* Freiburg 1998, p. 59.
27. Rudolf Steiner: GA 202, Dornach 1993, p. 256.
28. Rudolf Steiner: GA 204, Dornach 1979, p. 106.
29. Rudolf Steiner: GA 198, Dornach 1984, p. 80.
30. Georg Groot had heard the lecture given to workmen at the Goetheanum on October 10, 1923, 'behind the wall'. In it, Rudolf Steiner talked, among other things, about the significance of carbon and nitrogen, but also about prussic or hydrocyanic acid and potassium cyanide, and the effect it had on human beings. He said in this context: 'If anthroposophical knowledge were to spread, then not a single human being would use potassium cyanide to poison another. They would not dream of it! The occurrence of cyanide poisoning is entirely the result of the materialistic world conception, because people believe that when you are dead you are dead, whether you suffer death by cyanide or by inner dissolution. But it is by no means the same thing! When you suffer death by inner dissolution, then the soul and spirit have to go on the usual path into the spiritual world; they go on living. But if they poison each other with cyanide, the soul has the intention of going along with it with every single particle of its body, and in particular, to spread itself out in nitrogen and disperse in the cosmos. That is a real death of soul and spirit. If only people were to know that the soul and spirit are the actual human being then they would say: we cannot possibly produce the frightful explosion that would take place, in every detail, over the whole cosmos if a person is poisoned with cyanide. For every single person who is poisoned with cyanide gets caught up in the wrong way in the stream going from the Earth to the sun. And then you ought to be able to see, if you had the right instruments, a slight explosion happening in the sun every time someone is poisoned with cyanide. And that has a bad effect on the sun. Human beings damage the cosmos and also the forces streaming from the sun to the Earth

when they poison themselves with cyanide. Human beings really do have an effect on the cosmos. When people use cyanide to poison each other they are actually ruining the sun! This is the case with every cyanide poisoning' (Rudolf Steiner: GA 351, Dornach 1988, p. 47). In his report on his conversation with Steiner on 18 October, Groot confirmed that he himself had said: 'As I could not imagine that a physical substance of material origin could have the kind of effect on the soul so that it remains under the influence of it even after death, I asked Rudolf Steiner this question, and he was prepared to give me an immediate reply. This is what he said: "The human etheric body is bound to the physical body by means of oxygen. The moment the cyanide enters the body the oxygen is changed into nitrogen. This tears up the etheric body and there is no recall. The hierarchies are still interested in saving the person, which is very difficult for them. Such a person will enter their next incarnation as a cripple, and this will take several incarnations to bring into balance." ' Georg Groot, 'Gespräch mit Rudolf Steiner' in Peter Selg (editor): *Anthroposophische Ärzte. Lebens- und Arbeitswege im 20. Jahrhundert*, Dornach 2000, p. 263.

31. Ibid., p. 263ff.

32. In connection with Anna Samweber. Quoted by Hella Wiesberger, 'Zusammenschau der Geschichte der Gesellschaftsproblematik 1923', in GA 259, Dornach 1991, p. 863.

33. Karl Lang: *Lebensbegegnungen*, Benefeld 1972, p. 67.

34. Quoted by Hella Wiesberger in GA 259, p. 847.

35. Anna Samweber: *Aus meinem Leben. Erinnerungen an Rudolf Steiner und Marie Steiner-von Sivers*, edited by Jakob Streit, Basel 1982, p. 44ff (English: *Memories of Rudolf Steiner*, Rudolf Steiner Press 1991).

36. See Peter Selg: *Rudolf Steiner's Intentions for the Anthroposophical Society*, Great Barrington, 2011.

37. See Peter Selg: 'Tode im Denken. Zur Entwicklung des Materialismus im 19. Jahrhundert' in: Peter Selg, *Michael und Christus, Studien zur Anthroposophie Rudolf Steiners*, Arlesheim 2010, p. 241–262.

38. Rudolf Steiner: GA 260, Dornach 1994, p. 270.

39. Rudolf Steiner: GA 233, Dornach 1991, p. 162.

40. Rudolf Steiner: GA 239. Dornach 1985, p. 267 onwards.

41. Quoted from Peter Selg: *Koberwitz, Pfingsten 1924, Rudolf Steiner und der Landwirtschaftliche Kurs*, Dornach 2009, p. 16f. (English: *The Agriculture Course*, Temple Lodge 2008).

42. Quoted from Hanna Vollmer: *Chronik 1924*, Gütersloh/München 2004, p. 38.

43. Eric Hobsbawm: *Das Zeitalter der Extreme. Weltgeschichte des 20. Jahrhunderts*, München 1995, p. 26 (English: *The Age of Extremes, The Short Twentieth Century 1914–1991*, Abacus 1995).

44. Ibid., p. 72.

45. Ibid., p. 73.

46. 'We need the word "unborn"; it must become as acceptable a word in our cultural languages as the word "immortal" is, which our languages already have' (Rudolf Steiner: GA 203, Dornach 1989, p. 274). See also: Peter Selg, *Unbornness, Human Pre-existence and the Journey Towards Birth*, SteinerBooks 2010.

47. Eric Hobsbawm, op. cit., p. 693.

48. See Mark Mazower: *Dark Continent, Europe's Twentieth Century*, Penguin 1999.

49. See Klaus Hornung, *Das totalitäre Zeitalter, Bilanz des 20. Jahrhunderts*, Frankfurt a. M., 1993.

50. Eric Hobsbawm: op. cit., p. 31.

51. Rudolf Steiner: GA 211, Dornach 1986, p. 206.

52. Sergei O. Prokofieff: *Die Begegnung mit dem Bösen und seine Überwindung in der Geisteswissenschaft, Der Grundstein des Guten*, Dornach 1989, p. 13 (English: *The Encounter with Evil*, Temple Lodge 1999).

53. Quoted from Eric Hobsbawm, op. cit., p. 15.

54. Ibid.

55. Ibid., p. 719 onwards.

56. Sergei.O. Prokofieff: *Die Begegnung mit dem Bösen und seine Überwindung in der Geisteswissenschaft*, p. 44 and 82 (English: *The Encounter with Evil*).

57. See Emanuel Zeylmans van Emmichoven: *Willem Zeylmans van Emmichoven*, Temple Lodge 2002.

58. Willem Zeylmans van Emmichoven: *Der Grundstein*, p. 96 (English: *The Foundation Stone*).

59. Willem Zeylmans van Emmichoven, ibid., p. 111.

60. Sergei O. Prokofieff: *Rudolf Steiner and the Founding of the New Mysteries*, Temple Lodge 1994, see Introduction 'How I Came to Write the Book . . .'.

61. Rudolf Steiner: GA 233, from p. 159.

62. Rudolf Steiner: GA 300a, Dornach 1995, from p. 163.

63. Rudolf Steiner: GA 9, Dornach 2003, p. 82 (English: *Theosophy*, Rudolf Steiner Press).

64. Ibid., p. 62.

65. Rudolf Steiner: GA 21, Dornach 1983, from p. 158.

66. Rudolf Steiner: GA 260a, p. 34.

67. See Peter Selg: *Vom Logos menschlicher Physis, Die Entfaltung einer anthroposophischen Humanphysiologie im Werk Rudolf Steiners*, Dornach 2006.

68. Ibid., Volume 2, from p. 579. See Peter Selg: 'Das Wesen des menschlichen Willens', in *Der Wille zur Zukunft*, Arlesheim 2011, p. 23–41.

69. 'In the Sun Region, everything that human beings had begun to feel good

intentions towards, even in the smallest way, become a reality that is beheld by the Exusiai, Dynamis and Kyriotetes. We are seen by the beings of the Sun Region in the light of the goodness in us, in our thinking, feeling and experiencing.' (Rudolf Steiner: GA 239 p. 102.)

70. Compare this with Peter Selg: *Unbornness* (SteinerBooks 2010).

71. 'The genuine I lives in the same cosmic sphere in which the true reality of our Will lives.' (Rudolf Steiner: GA 179, Dornach 1993, p. 91.)

72. Rudolf Steiner: GA 26, Dornach 1998, p. 178.

73. See Peter Selg: *The Fundamental Social Law, Rudolf Steiner on the Work of the Individual and the Spirit of Community*, SteinerBooks 2011.

74. Rudolf Steiner: GA 260, p. 62.

75. To the 'unborn ones' in feeling and will, to their after-death experience, see in particular Rudolf Steiner: GA 153, Dornach 1997, from p. 113 on.

76. Willem Zeylmans van Emmichoven: *Der Grundstein*, p. 30 (English: *The Foundation Stone*).

77. See Peter Selg: *Vom Logos menschlicher Physis, Die Entfaltung einer anthroposophischen Humanphysiologie im Werk Rudolf Steiners*, Volume 2, from p. 604ff.

78. See Rudolf Steiner: GA 10, Dornach 1992, p. 34ff.

79. Georg Wilhelm Friedrich Hegel: *Phänomenologie des Geistes*, Volume 3, Frankfurt am Main 1986, p. 36.

80. Rudolf Steiner: GA 260, p. 62.

81. Rudolf Steiner: GA 40, Dornach 2005, p. 21.

82. Rudolf Steiner: GA 257, Dornach 1989, p. 76.

83. See Peter Selg: *Vom Logos menschlicher Physis, Die Entfaltung einer anthroposophischen Humanphysiologie im Werk Rudolf Steiners*, Volume 2, p. 572ff.

84. Rudolf Steiner: GA 1, Dornach 1987, p. 125ff.

85. It is in this way (from the periphery of the limbs to the head) that the higher members of man's being enter again every morning into their connection with the body, enabling an awakening to take place, 'from below upwards', as Rudolf Steiner described in detail. (See Rudolf Steiner: GA 239, p. 238ff.) In this connection see also Rudolf Grosse: 'Die Grundstein-Meditation' in *Die Weihnachtstagung als Zeitenwende*, p. 150f. (English: *The Christmas Foundation; Beginning of a New Cosmic Age*, Steiner Book Centre 1984).

86. Rudolf Steiner: GA 3, Dornach 1980, p. 90.

87. See Peter Selg: *Der Wille zur Zukunft*, Arlesheim 2011.

88. Rudolf Steiner: GA 260, p. 62ff.

89. Rudolf Steiner: GA 26, Dornach 1998, p. 14.

90. See in this connection (regarding the originally intended human bodily members restored again by Christ, and which go back to the evolutionary process of 'Old' Saturn): Sergei O. Prokofieff: *Rudolf Steiner und die*

Grundlegung der Neuen Mysterien, p. 308ff. (English: *Rudolf Steiner and the Founding of the New Mysteries*).

91. Statement by the discoverer of the DNA double helix, James Watson. Quoted by Hans-Jörg Rheinberger, 'Molekulare Genetik als Paradigma? Gentechnologie im Blick von Wissenschaftstheorie und medizinischer Ethik' in: Heinz Schott (editor): *Meilensteine der Medizin*, Dortmund 1996, p. 555. See also Peter Selg: 'Die geistige Dimension des Menschen? Zur Entwicklung der medizinischen Anthropologie im 20. Jahrhundert' in: Peter Heusser / Peter Selg, *Das Leib-Seele-Problem, Zur Entwicklung eines geistgemäßen Menschenbildes in der Medizin des 20. Jahrhunderts*, Arlesheim 2011, p. 82f.

92. Willem Zeylmans van Emmichoven: *Der Grundstein*, p. 38 (*The Foundation Stone*).

93. Rudolf Steiner: GA 260, p. 63.

94. See Sergei O. Prokofieff: *Die Grundsteinmeditation, Ein Schlüssel zu den neuen christlichen Mysterien*, p. 42 (English: *The Foundation Stone Meditation*).

95. See Peter Selg: *Vom Logos menschlicher Physis. Die Entfaltung einer anthroposophischen Humanphysiologie im Werk Rudolf Steiners*, Volume 2, p. 81ff., and Peter Selg: *Mysterium cordis, Aristoteles — Thomas von Aquin — Rudolf Steiner*, Dornach 2006, p. 129ff.

96. Ibid., p. 130.

97. Willem Zeylmans van Emmichoven: *The Foundation Stone*, from p.79 onwards.

98. See also Rudolf Steiner: GA 148, Dornach 1992, from p. 20 on.

99. Willem Zeylmans van Emmichoven, *Der Grundstein*, p. 52 (English: *The Foundation Stone*).

100. Rudolf Steiner: GA 260, p. 209.

101. Rudolf Steiner: GA 26, p. 116.

102. Rudolf Steiner: GA 257, p. 13.

103. See Sergei O. Prokofieff: *Menschen mögen es hören, Das Mysterium der Weihnachtstagung*, p. 733 (English: *May Human Beings Hear It! The Mystery of the Christmas Conference*).

104. Willem Zeylmans van Emmichoven: *Der Grundstein*, p. 37 (English: *The Foundation Stone*).

105. Rudolf Steiner: GA 40, p. 156.

106. Hermann Poppelbaum: 'Beiträge zum Verstehen der Grundsteinsprüche 1923' in Sergei O. Prokofieff (editor): *Die Grundsteinmeditation als Schulungsweg, Das Wirken der Weihnachtstagung in 80 Jahren*, p. 33.

107. 'Everything that goes beyond the human being is what we have on Earth as religion. The human ideal is what we have, beyond in the spiritual world, as religion. We are learning to understand that the various beings of the different spiritual hierarchies put their intentions, their forces, together so

that in the world stream, in the way it is described in my *Occult Science*, human beings are gradually coming into existence. The gods hold up in front of them, as the goal of their creation, the kind of human ideal that in no way resembles what physical man is now, but what could exist as the highest human life of soul and spirit, in the fully developed state of a human being. This image of humankind hovered then, as the highest ideal, as the religion of the gods, there before them. And, as though on the far shore of spiritual existence, the gods see hovering before them the temple that represents in the image of man, the highest artistic achievement of the gods' (Rudolf Steiner: GA 153, p. 97). This 'image of divine Being in the image of man' is that (sevenfold) man who has developed his highest spiritual members (spirit self, life spirit and spirit man) and unites in his being, in his spiritual body, the active forces of the hierarchies, as Willem Zeylmans van Emmichoven and Sergei O. Prokofieff were able to elaborate so convincingly in their Foundation Stone studies. Prokofieff's writings on these observations, from the year 1982, ended with the statement: 'The Foundation Stone meditation is the earthly/cosmic image of sevenfold man, who is filled with the Christ, of the human being who is coming from the World past to the World future, and in the present World period can find the Christ in this way in the present' (*Rudolf Steiner und die Grundlegung der Neuen Mysterien*, p. 333 — English: *Rudolf Steiner and the Founding of the New Mysteries*.) In his later publications, among other things, Prokofieff worked on this aspect of the ideal of the human being in the Foundation Stone and its connection with the resurrection body of the Christ and 'spiritual communion' in the individual. See among others: *Menschen mögen es hören, Das Mysterium der Weihnachtstagung*, p. 695ff. (English: *May Human Beings Hear It!*).

108. Friedrich Hölderlin: 'Patmos' in *Sämtliche Werke und Briefe*, Munich edition, Volume 1, Munich 1992, p. 449ff.

109. Rudolf Steiner: GA 78, Dornach 1986, p. 150.

110. 'It is necessary, above all where our present culture is concerned, that we increasingly acquire, through the effects of spiritual science on us, a new knowledge of Christ. And there are many things these days that are an official part of Christianity yet are so antagonistic to the character of Christ. It is essential that we acquire a greater and greater understanding of what our culture requires — a schooling in selflessness. A renewing of morality, a deepening of human moral life, can only come about by means of a training in selflessness. Human beings can only go through the school of selflessness in accordance with our present cycle of time by acquiring a thorough understanding of real selflessness. Going through world evolution, we can see no deeper understanding for selflessness than the one that has been given by Christ's own appearance on Earth. And to understand

the Christ means going through the school of selflessness. To know the Christ means getting to know all those impulses of humanity's evolution that seep into our souls so that they bring into our unselfish inclinations a glow, a warmth, a call to activating our souls — to unselfishness. Under the influence of materialism human unselfishness was lost in a certain way, which will only be understood by humanity in future times. But by means of entering deeply into a feeling for the Mystery of Golgotha, by acquiring a deep knowledge of the Mystery of Golgotha with our whole feeling, our whole soul being, we will be able once more to acquire a culture of self-lessness. And we can say: What Christ has done for Earth evolution covers the whole basic principle of selflessness, and what he can become for a conscious evolution of the human soul is a schooling in selflessness. We shall be aware of this best of all if we consider the Mystery of Golgotha in all its aspects' (Rudolf Steiner, GA 152, Dornach 1990, p. 151ff. See also Peter Selg: *The Culture of Selflessness, Rudolf Steiner, the Fifth Gospel and the Time of Extremes*, SteinerBooks 2012.)

111. Rudolf Steiner: GA 148, p. 64.
112. Willem Zeylmans van Emmichoven: *Der Grundstein*, p. 62 (English: *The Foundation Stone*).
113. Ibid., p. 61.
114. With the first publication of his *Rudolf Steiner and the Founding of the new Mysteries* Sergei O. Prokofieff had worked out that the call to the 'human soul' by the Christ comes about if one turns to him; and he writes there among other things: 'By means of this meditation he gives (to the human soul) a comprehensive understanding of his Being, awakens the will, in the name of the birth of a new human being in oneself, to work at transforming one's will, feeling and thinking.' See: *Rudolf Steiner und die Grundlegung der Neuen Mysterien*, p. 303 (English: *Rudolf Steiner and the Founding of the New Mysteries*).
115. Rudolf Steiner: GA 131, Dornach 1988, p. 70.
116. See Rudolf Grosse, *Die Weihnachtstagung als Zeitenwende*, p. 156ff. (English: *The Christmas Conference*), as well as the trail-blazing Christological studies of Sergei O. Prokofieff, *The Mystery of the Resurrection in the Light of Anthroposophy*, Temple Lodge 2010.
117. Willem Zeylmans van Emmichoven: *Der Grundstein* (*The Foundation Stone*) p. 11 and 78. '[...] The Christ addresses himself solely to the innermost being of man, his eternal, immortal core, which invisibly connects every single person to humanity as a whole. The Christ addresses himself to the community of the future [...] where "no one can be happy if someone else is unhappy". This founding of the new community, of the "new Earth" is the chief task of a humanity that has taken into itself the Christ as its higher ego, and transformed itself into a single living organism filled and ensouled

by the Christ' (Sergei O. Prokofieff: *Rudolf Steiner und die Grundlegung der Neuen Mysterien*, p. 327 — English: *Rudolf Steiner and the Founding of the new Mysteries*).

118. Willem Zeylmans van Emmichoven: *Der Grundstein* (*The Foundation Stone*), p. 77.

119. Ibid., p. 81.

120. Linking up with Rudolf Steiner's Cologne and Berlin descriptions given in May 1912, about the soul/spiritual 'sheaths' in connection with Christ's second coming (see GA 133 and GA 143), Sergei O. Prokofieff pointed out, for the first time, that the developing of the 'physical' conscience 'sheath' of Christ has a close connection with those processes that are referred to in the microcosmic will-verse of the Foundation Stone meditation, the development of the 'etheric' compassion and love 'sheath' with the processes of the microcosmic feeling-verse, and the developing of the 'astral' sheath, which has to be acquired from out of the forces of astonishment and wonder for the spirituality of the cosmos (or the cosmic 'World Thoughts'), with the third microcosmic thinking-verse (p. 328 — English: *Rudolf Steiner and the Founding of the new Mysteries*).

121. Rudolf Steiner: GA 260, p. 65.

122. Ibid., p. 208.

123. Ibid., p. 253.

124. Sergei O. Prokofieff: *Rudolf Steiner und die Grundlegung der Neuen Mysterien*, p. 318 (English: *Rudolf Steiner and the Founding of the New Mysteries*).

Bibliography

All quotations from Rudolf Steiner have been translated from the original German sources. A list of referenced works that have been published in English as complete 'GA' (*Gesamtausgabe* or Collected Works) titles are given below.

GA 1   *Nature's Open Secret*
GA 3   *Truth and Knowledge*
GA 9   *Theosophy*
GA 10   *Knowledge of the Higher Worlds* or *How to Know Higher Worlds*
GA 21   *Von Seelenrätseln* (extracts appear in *The Case for Anthroposophy*)
GA 26   *Anthroposophical Leading Thoughts*
GA 40   *Wahrspruchworte*
GA 78   *Fruits of Anthroposophy*
GA 131   *From Jesus to Christ*
GA 133   *Earthly and Cosmic Man*
GA 143   *Erfahrungen des Übersinnlichen. Die drei Wege der Seele zu Christus*
GA 148   *The Fifth Gospel*
GA 152   *Approaching the Mystery of Golgotha*
GA 153   *Inner Nature of Man and the Life Between Death and Rebirth*
GA 179   *Geschichtliche Notwendigkeit und Freiheit. Schicksalseinwirkungen aus der Welt der Toten*
GA 182   *Death as Metamorphosis of Life*
GA 198   *Heilfaktoren für den sozialen Organismus*
GA 202   *Der Mensch in Zusammenhang mit dem Kosmos*
GA 203   *Die Verantwortung des Menschen für die Weltentwickelung durch seinen geistigen Zusammenhang mit dem Erdplaneten und der Sternenwelt*
GA 204   *Materialism and the Task of Anthroposophy*
GA 211   *The Sun Mystery and the Mystery of Death and Resurrection*
GA 233   *World History in the Light of Anthroposophy*
GA 239   *Karmic Relationships*, Vols. V and VII
GA 240   *Karmic Relationships*, Vols. VI and VIII
GA 257   *Awakening to Community*
GA 259   *Das Schicksalsjahr 1923 in der Geschichte der Anthroposophischen Gesellschaft: Vom Goetheanumbrand zur Weihnachtstagung*
GA 260   *The Christmas Conference for the Foundation of the General Anthroposophical Society 1923–1924*
GA 260a   *Die Konstitution der Allgemeinen Anthroposophischen Gesellschaft und der Freien Hochschule für Geisteswissenschaft. Der Wiederaufbau des Goetheanum*

GA 264   *From the History and Contents of the First Section of the Esoteric School 1904–1914*

GA 300a   *Faculty Meetings with Rudolf Steiner*

GA 351   *Mensch und Welt. Das Wirken des Geistes in der Natur. Über das Wesen der Bienen*

Please check Rudolf Steiner Press (UK) www.rudolfsteinerpress.com and SteinerBooks (USA) www.steinerbooks.org for availability.

Books in English Translation by Peter Selg

On Rudolf Steiner:
Rudolf Steiner and Christian Rosenkreutz (2012)
Rudolf Steiner as a Spiritual Teacher: From Recollections of Those Who Knew Him
(2010)

On Christology:
The Creative Power of Anthroposophical Christology (with Sergei Prokofieff) (2012)
Christ and the Disciples: The Destiny of an Inner Community (2012)
Rudolf Steiner and the Fifth Gospel: Insights into a New Understanding of the Christ Mystery (2010)
The Figure of Christ: Rudolf Steiner and the Spiritual Intention behind the Goetheanum's Central Work of Art (2009)
Seeing Christ in Sickness and Healing (2005)

On General Anthroposophy:
The Culture of Selflessness: Rudolf Steiner, the Fifth Gospel, and the Time of Extremes (2012)
The Mystery of the Heart: The Sacramental Physiology of the Heart in Aristotle, Thomas Aquinas, and Rudolf Steiner (2012)
Rudolf Steiner and the School for Spiritual Science, The Foundation of the First Class (2012)
The Fundamental Social Law: Rudolf Steiner on the Work of the Individual and the Spirit of Community (2011)
The Agriculture Course, Koberwitz, Whitsun 1924: Rudolf Steiner and the Beginnings of Biodynamics (2010)
The Path of the Soul after Death: The Community of the Living and the Dead as Witnessed by Rudolf Steiner in his Eulogies and Farewell Addresses (2010)
Rudolf Steiner's Intentions for the Anthroposophical Society: The Executive Council, the School for Spiritual Science, and the Sections (2011)

On Anthroposophical Medicine and Curative Education:
I am for going ahead: Ita Wegman's Work for the Social Ideals of Anthroposophy (2012)
Karl König: The Child with Special Needs: Letters and Essays on Curative Education (Ed.) (2009).
Ita Wegman and Karl König: Letters and Documents (2009)
Karl König: My Task: Autobiography and Biographies (Ed.) (2008)
Karl König's Path to Anthroposophy (2008)

On Child Development and Waldorf Education:

I Am Different from You: How Children Experience Themselves and the World in the Middle of Childhood (2011)

The Essence of Waldorf Education (2010)

Unbornness: Human Pre-existence and the Journey toward Birth (2010)

A Grand Metamorphosis: Contributions to the Spiritual-Scientific Anthropology and Education of Adolescents (2008)

The Therapeutic Eye: How Rudolf Steiner Observed Children (2008)

Ita Wegman Institute

for Basic Research into Anthroposophy

Pfeffinger Weg 1 A CH-4144 Arlesheim, Switzerland
www.wegmaninstitut.ch
e-mail: sekretariat@wegmaninstitut.ch

The Ita Wegman Institute for Basic Research into Anthroposophy is a non-profit research and teaching organization. It undertakes basic research into the lifework of Dr. Rudolf Steiner (1861–1925) and the application of Anthroposophy in specific areas of life, especially medicine, education, and curative education. The Institute also contains and cares for the literary estates of Ita Wegman, Madeleine van Deventer, Hilma Walter, Willem Zeylmans van Emmichoven, Karl Schubert, and others. Work carried out by the Institute is supported by a number of foundations and organizations and an international group of friends and supporters. The Director of the Institute is Prof. Dr Peter Selg.